play • listen • appreciate • rest

Praise for *The 4 Habits of Joy-Filled Marriages*

A life-giving, relational "dietary supplement" for increased connection, resilience, and joy in any married couple's relationship! Marcus and Chris have made the brain science easy to "swallow" and the dosing very doable. Warning: The exercises laid out in this book are known to cause increased levels of oxytocin, dopamine, and serotonin in those married couples who practice them. Greater intimacy, more satisfying rest, more frequent laughter and joy are the most common side effects. Be aware that joy, in full strength, is extremely contagious and habit-forming.

LYN WALKER *Women's Ministries Coordinator, Community Reformed Church*

Fifteen minutes can transform your marriage. Chris and Marcus show how four simple rhythms can shape the course of your life together and increase the quality of your interactions. Engaging stories inspire you and create understanding while practical exercises support each habit informed by brain science. I love how Chris and Marcus begin the habits with Play; such a brilliant way to start! And if couples were able to create the habit of Listening for emotion, they would put us therapists out of business and I would gladly welcome that. This chapter alone is worth the price of the book. The list of couples I want to share this with is already too long. I can already imagine many small groups will utilize this book to enrich their marriages, families, and community. If you want to change your marriage in fifteen minutes a day, pick up this book. We wholeheartedly recommend this book because *the best relationships are built on the willingness to stay in the conversation.* This book will support your willingness.

JOHN AND SUNGSHIM LOPPNOW *Authors and creators of Presence and Practice*

The message and exercises within this book will transform marriages around the world! Marcus and Chris brilliantly take God's design of the brain and bond it with God's purpose for marriage. It's a wonderful, short, practical, and powerful read. Shorten the gaps between your joy and PLAN on an enriched, cherished marriage! This will now be the first book on marriage and life I recommend to friends.

DAVE MEAD *Executive Coach*

This is the book we've all been waiting for! The blend of brain science concepts with practical application makes this book a priceless gift for every marriage. I will be using this book as a daily guide in my own marriage and will have it stocked on the shelves of my office for the clients I serve. As a wife and a therapist, I'm so thankful for this amazing resource.

MONICA MOUER *MS, LPCS, CSAT, Certified EMDR Therapist*

If you are looking for a practical, not pie-in-the-sky, approach to growing your marriage, I strongly recommend this book! Marcus and Chris have written a book filled with simple, easy-to-follow guidelines to make relationships thrive! *The 4 Habits of Joy-Filled Marriages* is rooted firmly in relational principles of neuroscience and identifies four essential habits that are characteristics of joy-filled marriages. Chris and Marcus's P.L.A.N. outlines strategies that help couples practically apply these principles to grow more joyful habits and stronger bonds. The abundance of practical exercises to help spouses grow these habits together is one of the book's greatest strengths. The step-by-step instructions for these exercises provide a blueprint for husbands and wives who want more joyful connection.

ED KHOURI *Author and President of Equipping Hearts*

My wife, Stasi, and I have been through it all, and I can tell you these guys are right—it's all about joy. You can get joy back in your marriage. Really. You can recover intimacy and even playfulness! Read this book!

JOHN ELDREDGE *Author of* Wild at Heart *and* Love and War
Founder of Ransomed Heart Ministries

The integrity of this book is honest and organized. The exercises enable us to experience practical and empowering baby steps forward. In short, the content will reorient your thinking and create skills that empower resilience and playfulness.

DIETRICH DESMARAIS *CEO and Founder of EWMI (Emotional Wealth Management Inc.) Emotional Intelligence Executive Coaching*

The 4 Habits of Joy-Filled Marriages is a practical look at what makes for a true and lasting "in love" experience in marriage. The emphasis on play and listening, appreciation and nurturing rhythm, is simple and inspiring. Chris and Marcus have boiled down the nineteen Brain Skills of THRIVE Training into four key habits that are game-changers in helping people to make the shift from fear to joy in their relationships. I have experienced first-hand the power of these habits in my own marriage. As I have practiced the exercises, I have experienced profound connection with my wife, moments of deep joy, and a total transformation of our relationship. Our minds can so easily forget that joy and intimate connection are what life is all about. We need books like this one, full of good stories, clear instruction and playful ways to practice simply being together and noticing one another, that can help us recapture and hold onto the joy for which we were made.

CHARLES SPOELSTRA *Discipleship Counselor, Grace Ministries International*

The 4 Habits of Joy Filled Marriages offers a simple focus on the active practices that make people glad to be married. I have known these two authors for almost twenty years. Chris works tirelessly to train others in relational skills that build joy and resilience. Marcus works just as hard to keep things simple and central to the transformation of character into the likeness of Christ. Now the two have come together to create a book that takes marriage relationships further than the communication willpower solutions can go. This guide to exercising our relational brain does what a weekend of inspiration cannot sustain by focusing on the four practices that build the best marriages. These are not marriages where nothing goes wrong but rather relationships where recovery comes quickly. Get your bounce back or perhaps find the bounce you never had!

E. JAMES WILDER *Neurotheologian and Life Model theoretician at Life Model Works International speaker and coauthor of* Rare Leadership

The authors confirm the conclusions from the Gottman research on marital satisfaction. Warner and Coursey help couples practice specific, joyful activities to implement that research in their marriages in simple, fun ways that only take fifteen minutes a day. The exercises are well described and very helpful for practicing the skills necessary for building a master marriage. Shrink the "joy gap" in your marriage by learning to connect to your beloved in these well-guided, easy-to-do activities—then watch your marriage thrive!

MISA LEONESSA GARAVAGLIA *Relationship Coach*

With *The 4 Habits of Joy-Filled Marriages*, Warner and Coursey have offered us a necessary tutorial on the underpinnings of those things on which our marriages depend. Read this book and watch your marriage bear witness to each other and to the world that the God of love is also the God of joy.

CURT THOMPSON *author of* The Soul of Shame *and* The Anatomy of the Soul

Marcus Warner *and* Chris Coursey

The 4 Habits of *Joy-Filled* Marriages

How 15 Minutes a Day Will Help You Stay in Love
• *Brain Science Hacks that Boost Your* •
Emotional, Spiritual and Physical Connection

NORTHFIELD PUBLISHING
CHICAGO

Details of some stories have been changed to protect the privacy of individuals.

Edited by Michelle Sincock
Interior design: Erik M. Peterson
Chris Coursey photo: Charles Spoelstra
Cover design: Faceout Studio
Cover illustration of hand copyright © 2018 by mhatzapa/Shutterstock (111642920). All rights reserved.

All websites and phone numbers listed herein are accurate at the time of publication but may change in the future or cease to exist. The listing of website references and resources does not imply publisher endorsement of the site's entire contents. Groups and organizations are listed for informational purposes, and listing does not imply publisher endorsement of their activities.

Library of Congress Cataloging-in-Publication Data

Names: Warner, Marcus, author. | Coursey, Chris, author.
Title: The 4 habits of joy-filled marriages : how 15 minutes a day will help
  you stay in love / Marcus Warner and Chris Coursey.
Other titles: Four habits of joy-filled marriages
Description: Chicago : Moody Publishers, [2019] | Includes bibliographical
  references.
Identifiers: LCCN 2018060571 (print) | LCCN 2019002030 (ebook) | ISBN
  9780802497758 (ebook) | ISBN 9780802419071
Subjects: LCSH: Marriage--Psychological aspects. | Couples--Psychology. |
  Interpersonal relations. | Marital quality.
Classification: LCC HQ734 (ebook) | LCC HQ734 .W3165 2019 (print) | DDC
  306.81--dc23
LC record available at https://lccn.loc.gov/2018060571

ISBN: 978-0-8024-1907-1

We hope you enjoy this book from Northfield Publishing. Our goal is to provide high-quality, thought-provoking books and products that connect truth to your real needs and challenges. For more information on other books and products that will help you with all your important relationships, go to www.moodypublishers.com or write to:

Northfield Publishing
820 N. LaSalle Boulevard
Chicago, IL 60610

5 7 9 10 8 6 4

Printed in the United States of America

We joyfully dedicate this book to our wives,
Brenda Warner and Jen Coursey.
It is a rare thing these days to have a life partner
you look forward to growing old with,
but that is where we both find ourselves—
joyful and secure in the anticipation of sharing
whatever life brings with the wives we love.

CONTENTS

INTRODUCTION

ONE OF THE MOST startling revelations to come out of the latest breakthroughs in brain science is the discovery that there is no more powerful motivator in life than joy. It is nearly universally recognized that your brain functions at its best when it is running on the fuel of joy.[1] Yet you may not have pinpointed joy as the key to marital bliss. This was certainly true of Steve and Rebekah, a young couple with a strained marriage.[2]

Much of Rebekah's life had been driven by an undercurrent of anxiety, and she was looking for answers. Over the years, she had spent money on books and seminars and had little to show for it. In many ways, her disillusionment and despair had only gotten worse. Her marriage was also getting worse. Steve and Rebekah both knew their situation needed work but, despite a few attempts to get help, the distance between them steadily increased. Both of them could see they were heading in the wrong direction fast.

As part of her search for help, Rebekah attended a conference on brain science and joy where Chris Coursey was one of the main speakers. The presenters claimed couples could increase the joy in their marriages in just fifteen minutes a day by doing exercises the presenters had developed based on the latest breakthroughs in brain science. Rebekah was intrigued but skeptical. On the one hand, the thought of more joy in her marriage was appealing. After all, who doesn't want that? On the other hand, the claim seemed hard to believe.

However, with their marriage on the line, Steve and Rebekah decided they had nothing to lose and started doing daily joy exercises together. They were surprised and increasingly excited to see how fifteen minutes of daily "joy practice" began to change them. Rebekah noticed a growing sense of hope as joy and peace softened her anxiety. Steve began to lower his guard and share his thoughts, fears, and struggles with his wife. Their tendency to react and argue diminished, and both were amazed to discover that being together was starting to be more fun than television, reading novels, and other more isolated forms of entertainment. The small steps they took to grow joy each day were changing the dynamics of their marriage. Their emotional capacity was increasing and improving.

JOY AND BRAIN SCIENCE

Your emotional capacity directly relates to joy. **Emotional capacity** can be thought of as your ability to bounce back from difficult emotions or hard situations. When you fall in love, your emotional capacity soars. The rush of joy gives you an emotional high that makes it feel like nothing can get you down. On the other hand, have you ever had days when your joy level was so low it felt like more than you could handle just to get out of bed? Joy is the key to emotional capacity. When you have lots of joy, life just works better.

When joy is high, your marriage also works better. We're guessing you didn't get married because you thought you would be miserable with the person you love. You got married because you thought you would have more joy with him or her. However, as you may have discovered, joy can be an elusive thing. Most of us have no idea what causes joy or how to revive it when it begins to fade. That is what this book is all about. Chris Coursey and I want to provide you with a clear path and a variety of brain science–based exercises that will help you build a joy-filled marriage.

HOW TO USE THIS BOOK

If you are looking to increase your intimacy and happiness together, this book may be just what you need to put some wind in your marriage sails. Even the best marriages can use a little guidance at times. We think you will find the content and exercises in this book an invaluable guide for taking your marriage to the next level.

We designed this book with chapters to read followed by exercises to practice. Unless otherwise noted, Marcus Warner wrote the chapters (so when you see "I" or "me" in the text, Marcus is writing). Chris Coursey developed the exercises. Beginning with chapter 4, each chapter has several recommended exercises to do throughout the week. Feel free to repeat exercises so that you do at least one each day or look in the chapter's corresponding appendix for additional exercises.

If you read this book and spend fifteen minutes a day for the next month doing these exercises, you will almost certainly begin to see changes for the better in your marriage. If you do them for sixty or ninety days, you will develop habits that make joy the new normal in your marriage. Men who have done these exercises faithfully with their wives have commonly reported feeling more secure and less anxious in their marriages. The same is true for women, who have reported feeling more highly valued and cared for by their husbands. You have to be careful though. One man who went through this process wrote, "I work from home and I had to cut back on the exercises because my wife and I found ourselves in bed too much during the day and I was not getting any work done!"[3] You've been warned.

CHAPTER 1

Shrink Your Joy Gap

THE STORY OF HOW my wife, Brenda, and I fell in love is not one of love at first sight. We knew each other for two years before we went on our first date. During that time, we didn't really think of each other in romantic terms. For starters, Brenda was in a serious relationship with someone else for most of that time. In addition, I was her professor, so Brenda was kind of off-limits. I started teaching college at the age of 25 and promised myself I would not date any of the students. The idea of a serious relationship with Brenda snuck up on me unexpectedly. It started when I launched a young adult group at my local church. Brenda was the spiritual life director for the students on campus and the leader of the chapel band, so I invited her to join our team. It wasn't long before I realized how much I looked forward to those planning meetings! That's when it hit me: "I think I'm starting to fall for this girl!" During those dating years, I remember how much joy I felt. We were falling in love, and it was a lot of fun.

THE JOY GAP

You may have heard that love is a choice. Strictly speaking, this is not true. Love is attachment. It is a bond you share through good times and bad. You can choose to do loving things. You can choose to do kind things. You cannot choose to feel love. However, the more joy you build into your marriage, the more that feeling of being "in love" will stay strong and grow.

> *Falling "out of love" is all about the absence of joy.*

Falling in love is all about joy. When you fall in love with someone, you experience a "joy explosion" in your brain that floods your body with hormones (like dopamine and oxytocin)[1] that make it hard not to smile. Couples who stay in love throughout their married lives are couples who excel at the art of keeping their joy levels high. The opposite is also true. Low joy couples are in trouble. Falling "out of love" is all about the absence of joy.

A **joy gap** is the length of time between moments of shared joy. But when too much time passes between moments of shared joy, a joy gap is created that makes you feel distant and alone in your marriage. The wider the joy gap becomes, the more likely it is for your problems (and everyone has them) to overwhelm you. Couples who let the joy gap get *too* wide struggle tremendously and start to feel hopeless about their marriage. Not only does the gap rob you of intimacy, but the gap begins filling with resentment, and bad habits can begin to form that keep you apart instead of bringing you together. You start to feel like you are "falling out of love." People rarely just wake up one morning to the thought, "I'm not in love anymore." It happens gradually as the gap between moments of shared joy grows wider and wider with too much pain, too much resentment, and too many bad habits in between.

Eleven years into our marriage, Brenda and I started to struggle. She felt like she was living on emotional scraps and getting my relational leftovers. It seemed like work never stopped, and when it did, I shut down and gave myself to entertainment. For the most part, I was either working, spending time with the kids, or watching TV. She was around but rarely the focus of my attention. Our joy gap was definitely growing.

I didn't notice how big the joy gap in our marriage was getting until Brenda and I went on a date that went terribly wrong. We were finishing our meal, and I was feeling rather proud of myself for taking a few hours to invest in the marriage, when Brenda dropped a relational bomb on me. She told me she was starting to feel desperate about the distance in our marriage. To help me get the point, she painted a word picture for me. She said she felt like she lived in a cave with prison bars across the front. Meanwhile I was standing in front of the cave facing away from her and focused on everyone else.

That picture should have made me feel compassion, but it didn't. Instead, I got mad. I felt wrongly accused! How could she think such a thing about me? Instead of showing compassion, I justified myself and defended my behavior. The night didn't end well. It was clear something was broken in our marriage, and I had no idea what it was. At that point, I had never heard of a joy gap.

Just when we needed it most, I became friends with Jim Wilder and discovered his profound teaching on brain science and joy. Brenda will tell you it was the best thing that ever happened to our marriage. Learning the brain science helped us understand why we reacted to each other in certain ways. Grasping the importance of joy and learning some tools for building it into our marriage gave us new tracks to run on. Brenda and I have been married for over 28 years. We are both in our fifties, and our kids are adults in their own right. It has been quite a ride, and we have learned how important it is to make joy a priority in our marriage. It isn't that we don't have problems, but we have learned how to recover and keep our relationship bigger than our problems.

One couple who came to Chris for help typifies the process. They were successful, busy, and burned out. In Chris's terms, the husband was particularly "crispy." In spite of their success in the workplace and the outward signs of living "the good life," their marriage was on the rocks. Chris listened to their story then got them started on a routine of joy exercises (many of which are in this book), and the results were phenomenal. The earthquake that was shaking their marriage and threatening to destroy it quieted significantly. Within a few weeks, they began to feel much more stable as a couple. Not only did their marriage improve, but the anxiety level of their children subsided noticeably as the entire family benefited from the difference. A little joy went a long way. The husband later told Chris that doing these exercises was, without a doubt, the turning point in his marriage.

These daily exercises have helped this couple form some new habits that have all but eliminated the joy gap in their marriage. With these new tools, they have built a lifestyle that helps them experience joy together every day. Joy has become the new normal in their marriage.

Most marriages could use more joy. Honestly, if you don't learn how to shrink the joy gap in your marriage, things could get ugly. The goal of this book is to introduce you to four habits that shrink the joy gap and make joy your default setting. To help you get there, we recommend reading the chapters (on your own or together) and then blocking out fifteen minutes every day to do the exercise for that day. Your marriage is *worth* fifteen minutes a day. It's time to dive in and start making joy the new normal.

MAKING A PLAN

My dad is a World War II veteran. He likes to tell me the story of a friend from college who proposed to his fiancée in a unique fashion. It was the 1940s, the war had just ended, and my dad returned home from serving in Patton's Third Army to get his degree at a small college in the farm country of Indiana. His buddy was an electronics whiz and used his skills to put together a very special plan for proposing to his girlfriend. One night after dinner, he took her for a walk across campus. He casually suggested they stop by the science lab because he had been working on a project he wanted her to see.

When they arrived at the lab, the young romantic flipped a switch on a control panel, and through the magic of electricity, a heart of red lights sprang to life on the wall at the end of the room. He then flipped another switch and a white arrow began to gleam brightly as if shot through the heart. Finally, he flipped another switch and electric lights spelled out the words, "Will you marry me?" Who could resist a proposal like that? She said yes.

What impressed me about this story was the preparation involved. The extra work my dad's friend did took a memorable event and made it unforgettable. He went the extra mile to make the experience special. All the planning and preparation demonstrated that he had been thinking about her and loved her enough to spend hours making that night something they could relive for years to come.

To a large extent, this is what romance is all about. It is taking the time to prepare to be together. Preparation means you have been thinking about the other person. Your heart and your mind have been dwelling on how to make your special person happy, how to bring him or her joy.

To help you make a plan for building more joy into your marriage, Chris and I have identified four habits of joy-filled marriages. To help you remember them, we arranged them into an acrostic that spells PLAN.

Play together
Listen for emotion
Appreciate daily
Nurture rhythm

We will spend the rest of the book explaining these habits and giving you exercises to help build them. For now, let me give you a quick introduction.

Habit 1: Play Together

I have some good friends who have been married for nearly fifty years. When I told them I was writing a book on the four habits of joy-filled marriages, the man leaned forward in his chair and said, "What's your first habit?" I could tell by the look in his eyes he knew what he wanted to hear. I said, "Our first habit is playing together." The man nearly jumped out of his chair. "Exactly!" He was beaming. "You have to play together and keep having fun. We have made that one of the top priorities in our marriage." It seems to have worked. They have raised twelve kids of their own and served as surrogate parents to dozens of other young people through the years.

I have known this couple for two decades, and they have one of the most joy-filled marriages I have seen and have raised some of the most joyful children I know. One of their secrets was their commitment to having fun together. They built their calendar around family trips. They constantly invited people to their home. We often weren't the only guests at the table when we visited them. It was clear from being around them that they worked hard and played hard and made relational joy a top priority for their family.

I also couldn't help but notice that this man was rubbing his wife's feet as we talked. Next to their faith in God, they both agreed that playing together was the key to being in love after a lifetime together.

Habit 2: Listen for Emotion

Left-brain people tend to listen for problems. Right-brain people listen for emotions. In a classic (fictitious) left-brain conversation, Anne tells her husband Tom about something important while he reads the newspaper, keeps tabs on the TV in the background, and eats his breakfast. At some point, Anne explodes, "Are you even listening to me? I feel like I'm talking to the wall!" At this, Tom calmly lowers his paper and, with a feeling of triumph, repeats back to her every word she just said. Anne is mystified but not really comforted. The reason Tom can do this is because he is listening to his wife with the problem-solving, left side of his brain. What he is *not* doing is tuning in to her by looking his wife in the eyes and listening for the emotions being expressed.

I have found that one of the most helpful pieces of advice for left-brain dominant people is to learn how to listen for emotions and not just problems. This helps keep your relational engine engaged. A woman approached me at a recent conference and asked, "What are emotions? How can I listen for emotions if I don't know what they are or how to identify them?" She went on to explain that she had spent her whole life managing relationships, doing damage control, and avoiding most emotions. If you can relate to this, then be sure to read chapter 5 on listening for emotion. We will explain six foundational emotions to listen for as you learn to build this skill.

Habit 3: Appreciate Daily

Not long after learning about the power of joy, a couple asked to meet with me about some issues in their marriage. I decided to try an experiment. After listening to their story and validating the emotions I was hearing, I asked them to take a moment and think about what they appreciated most about the other person. Specifically, I asked, "When you were first attracted to this person, what did you most admire or respect about them?" I then had them pivot toward each other, hold hands, make eye contact, and share their feelings of appreciation. There was just one rule when sharing appreciation: they couldn't use the word "but." They couldn't say, "I really admire the way you love our kids, but I wish you wouldn't . . ." Adding a "but" to the expression of appreciation pulls the rug out from under it.

With this ground rule in place, they did the exercise, and the results were shocking. They went from barely looking at each other, sitting on opposite sides of the room, to snuggling so close I had to tell them not to start kissing. Shared joy can be a powerful thing, and appreciation is one of the most powerful habits you can form for building joy.

Habit 4: Nurture Rhythm

Life can be hectic. It is easy for your marriage to turn into a business partnership. Sometimes we spend all our time cleaning, working, organizing, parenting, and crashing. We don't have a rhythm to life that creates margin. Instead, we have a rhythm that creates distance in our marriage and burn-out in many areas of our lives. Couples who share joy on a daily basis generally have healthy marriages. It is essentially impossible to have sustained joy in your marriage without a rhythm that includes rest.

Couples who nurture rhythm by incorporating times of resting together, as well as playing together, create a foundation for joy that is sustainable for years to come. One couple I know always sits on the back deck together for half an hour or more in the evening and watches the sun set. Another couple plays cards every evening before bed. Habits we develop that allow us to rest together create security in our relationship and promote the kind of rhythm that helps us keep our love fresh.

SHRINKING THE GAP

As part of helping you shrink the joy gap in your marriage, we want to introduce you to some of the brain science behind joy. Brain science may sound technical and a bit boring to some (or perhaps exciting to others), but we will do our best to keep things simple and practical. We want you to understand enough about how the brain operates to give you a picture of why joy is so important and how it grows.

CHAPTER 2

The Brain Science Behind Joy

IN THIS CHAPTER we want to introduce you to four breakthroughs in brain science that have made joy a growing point of emphasis in everything from addiction recovery and PTSD treatments to leadership, parenting, and, of course, marriage.[1] Joy and the brain science behind it are transforming the field of psychology and have found their way into the curriculum at most major universities.[2]

Since most of what we are teaching in this book is based on brain science, we want to help you understand some basics before we go too far. We are going to focus on four significant breakthroughs that explain the role of joy in the brain.

BREAKTHROUGH 1: THE BRAIN MAGNET

The deepest, most primal part of your brain is like a magnet. It is often called the attachment center of the brain.[3] The discovery of the attachment center has led to widespread interest in attachment theory and its application to all sorts of issues.

Joyful attachment is the most powerful motivator in life.

The **brain magnet** is a term we created to describe your drive to bond with other people. You come out of the womb craving attachment. The force inside you that wants to bond with others is so deep that, from your brain's perspective, nothing is more important than attachment. As a result, no pain is greater than attachment pain and no joy is greater than attachment joy. Experiences like the death of a loved one, divorce, or separation from people we love can create incredibly deep pain. On the other hand, people will cross deserts, climb mountains, and fight wars to be with the people they love.

One of the key discoveries of brain science is that Freud was wrong. He taught that the fear of death and desire for sex were the most powerful motivators in the world. However, the discovery of the brain magnet has shown that attachment—specifically, joyful attachment—is the most powerful motivator in life. For the sake of joyful attachment, people will abstain from sex and face their fears, even the fear of death. Mothers have lifted cars off trapped children. Men have wrestled sharks to save friends. People enter fiery buildings, face certain death, and endure incredible pain because the attachment they feel to someone is deeper than any other power in life.

Fear Bonds and Joy Bonds

The challenge here is that your brain can bond in one of two ways. It can bond in joy or it can bond in fear. When I was a kid, I remember getting a set of Scottie dog magnets in my Christmas stocking. One dog was white and one was black. Each had a magnet on the bottom. When you faced the dogs toward each other, the magnets made them slide together. This made their noses touch, and it looked like the dogs were kissing. Part of the fun was seeing how far apart you could move the dogs and still get them to slide together and "kiss." The other part of playing with these Scottie dog magnets was turning their tails toward each other. When you did this, the same magnetic force that had caused them to "kiss" now pushed them away from each other. If you tried to force the tails to touch, you could feel the magnetic energy at work as the dogs repelled each other. This illustrates the difference between joy bonding and fear bonding. When two people bond in joy, there is a positive energy that attracts them to each other. When two people bond in fear, negative energy repels attraction.

A **joy bond** is characterized by several key traits:

- Lots of smiles
- Positive feelings from being together (or even thinking about being together)
- The security to act like yourself around the other person
- An ability to connect safely at an emotional level
- The sense that you are with "your people"

A **fear bond** looks quite different:

- Smiling is rare
- Hiding emotions is common
- Wearing masks for fear that people will not be happy to see you if you act like yourself
- Isolation becomes normal
- Shutting down when problems arise and losing the desire to be relational
- Treating someone who should be a friend more like an enemy

It is possible to switch back and forth between a fear bond and a joy bond with the same person. When you are acting like your relational self, you tend to bond in joy. When you get triggered or when you are disengaged relationally, you are much more likely to experience a fear bond. However, most of us have an established pattern to our relationships. One of the goals of this book is to help you recognize when you are "fear bonding" to one another and begin to build the habits that can transform your relationship.

I have met with many couples through the years who were fear bonded to each other. Some of them lived together for decades, but they lived largely separate lives. Some stayed married but fought constantly. I have also known several couples who were clearly joy bonded. Their home had a positive energy that made you enjoy being there.

The Joy Bucket—*Joy/Identity Center*

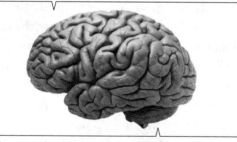

The Brain Magnet—*Attachment Center*

BREAKTHROUGH 2: THE JOY BUCKET

The magnet of attachment is located at the base of your brain, and the joy center (or joy bucket) is at the top of your brain. While you are in the womb, your brain grows from the bottom up. The last parts of your brain don't fully develop until after you are born. Once your brain reaches your skull, it begins to curve forward toward the front of your head. Therefore, the front of your brain is also the top of your brain.[4] We call it the **joy bucket** because this important center in your brain grows with the experience of joy. One of the great things about the joy bucket is that it has the capacity to grow for as long as you live. This means that you always have the ability to grow more joy no matter how little joy you have lived with until now.

By filling your joy bucket to capacity again and again, you grow that part of your brain. The more regularly you experience joy with other people, the larger your joy bucket gets. It is hard to overstate how important it is to grow a large joy bucket. The bigger it gets, the more emotionally and relationally secure you become. A large joy center will make it easier to navigate the ups and downs of marriage.

The size of your joy bucket is crucial to how much emotional capacity you have. You can think of emotional capacity as a bridge. You wouldn't want to drive a semitruck across an old wooden bridge from the 1800s. The bridge simply wouldn't have the capacity to handle the weight. In the same way, your capacity to handle the weight of life's problems directly relates to your capacity to live with joy and return to joy after experiencing upset emotions. Joy keeps our relationships intact even when there are problems or upsetting emotions present.

This is one reason why joy exercises are so important. By doing joy exercises together for fifteen minutes each day, you literally grow your capacity for joy, which increases your emotional resilience, your attachment to one another, and your confidence in who you are.

BREAKTHROUGH 3: THE ON/OFF SWITCH

When I lead marriage retreats, I often tell people to imagine they have a switch on the back of their necks. When this switch is on, the relational circuitry in your brain turns on. This allows you to stay anchored and present and remember what is important about your relationship even when things get hard. However, when your switch is off, your relational circuits shut down. When this happens, you lose your ability to live with joy, and people become problems to solve rather than people to love. This happens because the right side of the brain contains your relational circuitry. When those circuits are on, you remain relational, act like yourself, return to joy from upset emotions, and endure hardships well.[5] The left side of the brain focuses on problem-solving and talking about problems. This is why sometimes talking about our problems amplifies the pain rather than resolving it.

My wife has often told me, "I really like relational Marcus. When your relational circuits are on, you're a pretty nice guy. But nonrelational Marcus is kind of scary." Why is that? When "nonrelational Marcus" shows up, it is usually because I have been triggered by a tone of voice, a feeling of being wronged, or something my wife has done. As a result, my switch flips to the "off" position, my relational circuits shut down, and I am left trying to handle my relationship without access to my relational brain.

You can tell when your switch goes off and your relational circuits shut down with four simple tests. I use the word CAKE to help me remember them. This acrostic also helps you know how to flip the switch and turn your relational circuits back on.

CURIOSITY. When your switch is off, you lose all curiosity about your spouse. You don't care what they think or how they feel because you are detached from that part of your brain. Your long history together has you convinced you have the other person figured out, and you might think you already know their thoughts or feelings. Without curiosity, you usually just want the other person to go away, stop talking, and leave you alone.

Flip the Switch. Once you realize that you have lost your curiosity and feel like you have the other person all figured out, you need to step away from the situation briefly. This may be as simple as looking away while you think of a way to show curiosity, or it may mean excusing yourself from the conversation until you can get your relational circuits back on. I have learned that when I lose my curiosity, it is because I have developed a narrative about how Brenda "always" acts. When this narrative controls my thinking, I only see those facts about her that fit the narrative. In other words, I remember all the true events that support the storyline of how she "always" acts. In order to find my curiosity, I have to get outside the narrative and look at some different facts. Once I have regained my curiosity, it is safe to continue the conversation.

APPRECIATION. With your switch in the off position, you can't remember what you appreciate about the person you love. Instead, you find it very easy to remember all the reasons you feel resentment. Appreciation produces attraction, so without appreciation, it is easy to feel resentment, find blame, and see the other person as an enemy.

Flip the Switch. To rediscover appreciation, you again need to disconnect briefly. The purpose of disconnecting is to focus on remembering what you appreciate about your partner. It helps to have a top ten list already put together of qualities you appreciate in him or her. I have also discovered that the more regularly I share appreciation with Brenda, the less resentment I feel. Appreciation also helps her act like herself, and I really like my wife when she acts like herself.

KINDNESS. With your circuits off, you don't feel like being kind. Instead, you feel like winning. When you only care about winning, kindness becomes a tool you use to get what you want. If curiosity and appreciation have shut down, kindness won't be far behind.

Flip the Switch. I have learned to go through a simple checklist of acts of kindness I know Brenda likes. This includes initiating holding her hand, telling her she is beautiful, giving her an item she has mentioned needing, or taking initiative around the house. These ideas were inspired by Gary Chapman's book *The 5 Love Languages*. One of the funny things about kindness is that whenever I'm intentional about it, and I see how Brenda responds, I always wonder why I'm not intentional more often.

EYE CONTACT. One sure sign your switch is off is that you stop making eye contact. The problem-solving part of your brain isn't relational, so when the relational part of your brain shuts down it is easy for problems to become bigger than relationships. Our goal is exactly the opposite. We want to keep relationships bigger than problems.

Flip the Switch. One of the simplest ways to jumpstart your relational brain is to make eye contact. Remembering to warmly look your wife or husband in the eyes will often remind you of the need for kindness, appreciation, and curiosity.

BREAKTHROUGH 4: THE NARRATIVE ENGINE

The brain magnet, the joy bucket, and the on/off switch are all related to activity on the right side of your brain.

This fourth breakthrough has to do with what is happening on the left side of your brain. I sometimes call the left side of the brain the "narrative engine." That is because this part of your brain spins narratives to help you explain life. My friend and board-certified psychiatrist Karl Lehman calls the narrative engine "the verbal logical explainer."[6] That is a mouthful, but it means the engine on the left side of your brain likes to find words to offer rational explanations to what you are experiencing.

For example, when I get into an argument with Brenda, the switch in my brain usually turns off, and my relational circuits shut down. My narrative engine tends to race with a storyline of how she "always" treats me like this. To support this narrative, I often recall events that seem to prove my point and reinforce the way I feel about her.

I remember one such fight. I shut down relationally and quit talking. I went into another room, and my narrative engine started working hard at creating a storyline that made Brenda the source of all my problems. However, in the middle of this meltdown, something strange happened. I think it was God. A new thought entered my head that didn't fit with the narrative I was creating. This thought said, "Be careful, Marcus. She is precious and fragile. Don't break her." Along with the new thought came a picture of a delicate china teacup. I recognized the significance of the metaphor, and within a matter of

What you believe about your wife or husband will have a profound effect on how you treat and feel about him or her.

moments, a new narrative about Brenda began to form in my mind. She wasn't a problem to be solved or a taskmaster making my life miserable. She was lovely and, yes, fragile, and deep down all she wanted was to be loved. As this new narrative took root, I could feel my relational circuits click back on. My appreciation returned, and I found myself wanting to be kind and gentle with her.

Narratives are powerful. What you believe about your wife or husband will have a profound effect on how you treat and feel about him or her. In marriage counseling situations, I have asked people to answer the following questions: "Are there lies you believe about your husband or wife that need to be exposed?" Then I ask, "What is the truth you need to focus on that will change the way you see them?" In Christian settings, I have people ask these questions in prayer form. They pray, "God, will you show me . . ."

Let me give you some examples. One woman saw her husband as a clown, another as a ball and chain keeping her from flying. One husband saw his wife as a monster who was ruining his life. You can see how pictures like these could stir up very negative emotions that would make it very hard to share intimacy or feel love.

Following this exercise, one husband came to me in tears and confessed that he had blamed all the problems in his marriage on his wife. He told me the picture he had seen of her was so terrible, he didn't want to share it. He then shared that God had given him a new picture of his wife and that he had seen himself in a new light as well. He had come to our marriage retreat hoping it would fix his wife. He was leaving determined to be a better husband because his narrative had changed.

SHRINKING THE GAP

There are more breakthroughs in brain science than we can discuss in one chapter,[7] but one final breakthrough is worth mentioning. The relational circuits in your brain are primarily composed of **mirror neurons**. As you can probably tell by the word "mirror," these neurons learn by watching other people in action and imitating those actions. This means you can't train the relational right side of your brain by reading a book and making better choices. You have to interact with another person in order to train your mirror neurons. This is why we didn't just write a few chapters on these habits and say, "Good luck." We have a training program included for you to practice with your spouse.

Doing the exercises in this book will not only help your marriage, it will grow your emotional capacity for life. That is a win/win. Learning the habits of joy-filled marriages can help you move past the fear-based bonding you may have learned growing up so you can begin to develop the habits practiced in joy-filled marriages.

CHAPTER 3

Why Joy Can Be So Hard to Find

JOY ISN'T SIMPLY a choice you make. Trying to choose joy can feel like trying to fall asleep when you have insomnia. Joy is a feeling you get when you are happy to be with someone who is happy to be with you. If you have grown up without a lot of relational joy, it is going to take some focused work before joy will become a habit. Even if you grew up in a relatively happy home, there are definitely forces that work against our efforts at living with joy. Let us introduce you to three of the most common obstacles to sharing joy with another person.

THE BUTTON DANCE

If you think of marriage as a dance, most of us start our marriages wanting to be as close to each other as possible.

Sometimes it can feel like we will never lose our joy because we are so in love. However, most marriages experience something I call the button dance. It works like this.

Imagine that you have a powder keg in your belly in which you keep all the pain and emotional baggage from your past. Now imagine that you have buttons covering the outside of your body with wires that connect them to this powder keg. As long as no one pushes your buttons, your issues stay nicely tucked away inside and things run smoothly. In fact, if you get really good at avoiding situations that push your buttons, you can start to feel like you don't have any issues.

However, sooner or later, everybody gets their buttons pushed, and when that happens, look out—things can get explosive in a hurry. When you push your partner's buttons and their powder keg erupts, it lets out a torrent of pent-up emotions. Stunned and confused by this outburst, you may feel like backing away from the other person and wonder to yourself, "Okay, who are you, and what happened to the person I married?"

When the powder keg erupts, something new enters the dance: fear. We aren't quite sure what triggered the eruption, but we know we don't feel as safe as we did before it happened. The more often we push each other's buttons, the more fear we feel in our marriage. As we mentioned in the last chapter, fear drives us apart and robs us of intimacy. We may stay in the dance, but we become masters of avoidance. Soon we learn there are issues that simply aren't safe to talk about, so we avoid them. As these topics and situations accumulate, our avoidance grows until we find that the joy gap in our marriage is starting to feel beyond hope. This is why you often see people who have stayed married for fifty years or more, but have a painful lack of intimacy in their marriage. They remain together, but the button dance has driven them into living separate lives. It is like watching someone try to grow a garden in a desert.

I spoke with one counselor who told me that in the early years of his marriage, he and his wife never fought. However, this wasn't a sign of a healthy marriage. It was a sign that they had become experts in avoidance. Eventually the button dance started, and their marriage became a miserable mess. Several years went by before they learned about the brain science of joy, but once they did, they began intentionally working on the skills being taught in this book. Today, they live with more joy in their marriage than either of them would have believed possible just a few years ago. It took some work, but they have stepped out of the button dance and into the habits that keep their joy high.

FEAR MAPPING

A second problem that works against sharing joy is fear mapping. This term refers to the habit we develop of scanning our environment for problems to fix instead of looking for blessings to appreciate. As we have seen, the brain can form two kinds of attachments: joy bonds and fear bonds. A **joy bond** is an attachment to someone in which we feel secure. A **fear bond** is an attachment in which we are never quite sure where we stand with the other person—or we are quite certain of where we stand, and it isn't good.

People who grow up with fear bonds (without secure attachments) learn how to fear map their world. They have trained their brains to look for whatever is scariest in their environment. As a result, they tend to fixate on problems to be solved and pain to be avoided. When pain and problems are the focus of your brain's activity, it is virtually impossible to grow joy.

In his bestselling book on marriage, John Gottman described the habits that distinguished "master marriages" from "disaster marriages." He defines a master marriage as one in which the relationship is still healthy after six years. A disaster marriage is one that either ended or was in serious trouble within six years.[1] In many ways, master marriages were characterized by the four habits in this book. Couples in "master marriages" were joy bonded. They had developed the habit of appreciation and entering into each other's joys. For example, if the wife showed excitement about her book club, the husband didn't just say, "That's nice" and keep watching TV. He would enter into the conversation and share his wife's joy about her book club.

In one marriage I know, the wife saw how much her husband loved NASCAR and decided to enter into that with him, even though she didn't know anything about it. She actually bought *The Complete Idiot's Guide to NASCAR* and *The History of NASCAR* before attending their first race together. It was a lot of fun for her as she began to realize that she knew more about the history of the sport than most of the die-hard fans surrounding them. This wasn't just a one-way street either. Her husband started watching HGTV in order to share his wife's love of home improvement. By consistently entering into one another's interests, the sphere of life they share together has grown, which has helped to shrink the joy gap in their marriage.

In some marriages, though, the habits of appreciation and sharing joy never develop. Instead, resentment and fear grow into habits. As we have already noted, when fear serves as your brain's default setting, you tend to develop some bad habits like avoidance ("I'd rather be texting on my phone or watching TV than talking to you"), anger ("It's your fault that I'm upset. I was perfectly happy watching TV and texting. Why do you have to be so needy?"), and addiction ("I can't wait until my first glass of wine," or "I just need to get away from all of this" as you search for porn on the internet).

The four habits taught in this book can help you overcome the practice of fear-mapping your world and help turn your marriage into a "master" marriage as well.

RESENTMENT

The longer the gap between moments of shared joy in your marriage, the more fertile the soil for resentment. If your marriage has been dominated by the button dance and fear mapping, you can guarantee that resentment has become a big issue.

If you think of the wrong done to you like a weight that is placed on a scale, forgiveness can feel very unjust, almost as though you're supposed supposed to take the weight off the scale and simply pretend nothing happened. It reminds me of a pastor who was called to the home of a couple because the man had just confessed to an affair with his wife's best friend. As the pastor drove to the home, his mind raced with the scenarios he might face and how he should handle them. The scenario he actually faced caught him off guard. The husband—who had just confessed to the affair—was angry. The adulterous man said, "Thank God you are here, pastor! Would you tell my wife to start acting like a Christian?" The pastor must have looked puzzled, because the husband continued, "I told her I was sorry. Now tell her to kiss and make up so we can put this whole thing behind us like nothing ever happened."

This adulterous husband was confused on several points. First, he didn't really seem to understand Christianity. He certainly didn't understand repentance or forgiveness. And based on what I can see in the story, he was likely a narcissist. Narcissists are unable to accept a shame message and they master the art of deflecting it to others. This is exactly what this man was doing. Rather than accept the shame of what he had done, he was deflecting shame back to his wife. Finally, he confused forgiveness with reconciliation. Reconciliation is about restoring trust and takes time. It takes two to reconcile. It only takes one to forgive. His wife offered forgiveness, which meant some form of reconciliation could begin. He was demanding reconciliation and calling it forgiveness.

Forgiveness doesn't mean there are no consequences for behavior. Parents understand this. We forgive our children constantly and still give them consequences for their actions. For example, you can forgive someone and still press charges against them so they don't hurt other people. You can forgive an alcoholic and still create boundaries and let them feel the consequences of their behavior.

Forgiveness, from a Christian perspective, is taking the weight of what has been done to you and giving it to God. At the heart of the process is a choice. It is choosing to allow God to be the judge rather than you, and letting God carry the weight rather than you. I sometimes explain this to people as turning the debt you are owed over to God's collection agency.

Healthy marriages are filled with forgiveness, not resentment. It is a way of saying, "I want our relationship to be bigger than our problems." We find peace when we see people as God sees them and discover people are more than the sum of their mistakes. Choosing to forgive and learning to see people as God sees them create a powerful one-two punch for dealing with resentment.

SHRINKING THE GAP

If you want a joy-filled marriage, you must build the habits that create joy. Habits are extremely powerful. In fact, I have a friend who wants to get a bumper sticker that says, "The one who dies with the best habits wins!"

From a brain science perspective, a habit forms through repetition. The more often you practice something, the more quickly your brain learns to see that activity as normal. Within thirty days, your brain will begin to rewire itself to adapt to this new normal. For example, going without coffee, sugar, or alcohol for thirty days usually breaks your brain's craving for it. If your new habit extends to sixty or ninety days, new pathways in your brain become fully formed and habits are established. You know that a habit has been created when you begin doing things without "choosing" to do them. Much like a reflex, they happen almost automatically.

Chris and I aren't suggesting you can fix all of your marriage problems by growing joy. However, habits are the practices that mold our lives and set the course for whether we will live with joy or fear in our marriage. Join us for a thirty-day journey of insights and exercises to help you jumpstart your PLAN for building the habits of a joy-filled marriage.

CHAPTER 4

Habit #1: Play Together

WHEN YOU FIRST started to date, my guess is that playing together came pretty naturally. A lot of couples go bowling, play miniature golf, attend parties or concerts, go to the beach, and play board games together. Trying to get creative is part of the fun of dating.

When Brian and Cathy started dating, Brian found out that Cathy had grown up figure skating. Wanting to do something that would touch her heart, he arranged to take her to a special open skating event at the legendary Joe Louis arena in downtown Detroit. She loved it so much, it became a common location for date nights. Cathy knew Brian was a huge fan of the Detroit Redwings hockey team, so she learned everything she could about hockey and they started going to the games together. They didn't stop with ice skating and hockey. Brian loved to fish, so Cathy agreed to go fishing even though it wasn't something she was used to doing. Cathy loved art, so Brian took her to art museums and began to learn about the history of art. By taking an interest in each other's passions, they found more and more ways to play together.

As life goes on, it is important not only to keep on playing together, but to expand the ways you play together by building new hobbies. Brenda has an aunt and uncle who live near a golf course. As her uncle entered into "semi-retirement," he joined a golf league and began spending more time at the course. It wasn't long before his wife decided to take some lessons so they could share this hobby together. Now they both enjoy watching golf on TV, and they play together a couple times a month during the summer. He still has his own golf league with the guys, but golf is now something they enjoy together.

The point is not what you do, but that you grow the list of ways that you can have fun sharing life together.

I know couples who have built new hobbies around snorkeling, making ceramics, bird watching, gardening, camping, wine tasting . . . the list goes on. The point is not *what* you do, but that you grow the list of ways that you can have fun sharing life together. It is okay for couples to have different hobbies, but you need some that you can do together as well.

In this chapter, we want to look at three practical ways to increase joy in your marriage through play: special events, relational sex, and social routines.

SPECIAL EVENTS

Shared hobbies, weekly dates, anniversary celebrations, and vacations give you something to anticipate together with joy, and they make memories you can share again and again. Sometimes anticipating the fun is better than the event itself.

For my thirtieth birthday, Brenda booked two nights at a bed and breakfast for us. She found a big farmhouse not far from Chicago that had sheep and llamas on the property. Part of the experience was getting to be around the animals and pet them (I think that was more for her than me!). She also rented a sports car for the occasion. I was in graduate school at the time, and we were driving a Ford Escort, so a sports car was a pretty cool addition to the experience.

Not everything went well on that trip. My birthday is in December, and we were living in the Chicago suburbs. On our way to the bed and breakfast, it started to snow. Instead of falling gently, the snow was pelting the car, driven by a biting north wind. About this time, I made my first mistake. I saw the sign for the bed and breakfast and turned at the next driveway. About two seconds later, we found ourselves stuck axle-deep in the mud.

I had turned onto an unfinished entrance that ended abruptly in a farm field. Since everything was covered with snow—and it was dark out—I couldn't tell what was happening until it was too late.

Suddenly, I found myself getting out of the car in my dress clothes while Brenda crawled over to the driver's position in her high heels and fancy dress. I had to push the car out of the mud while the snow collected on my frozen face and Brenda revved the engine of our sports car, coating me in mud and slush. It took several minutes as we rocked the car back and forth—just long enough to become really miserable—but eventually our efforts paid off, and we got back on the road. While my face was icing over, I can't say I was really enjoying the experience. But we got warmed up, dried off, and ended up having a great weekend together.

I must confess that more than once, my anniversary celebrations have consisted of little more than taking Brenda to a slightly nicer restaurant than usual. However, anniversaries provide great opportunities to build intimacy and have some fun. For example, you might write a poem or a letter for your husband or wife. It can be funny, nostalgic, or romantic. I have a friend who writes his wife a poem nearly every anniversary. Perhaps that felt right to me because my dad often wrote poems for my mom and for us kids on special occasions. Taking time to write a poem shows preparation and adds to the romance of the moment.

Another way to add meaning to any special occasion is to make something creative. My dad used to make my mom a piece of furniture every Christmas. He worked at a college and used the wood shop there. My mom had a nice hutch she loved to work at, an old-fashioned dry sink, a table especially made for the entry to the house, and a few other pieces made with love and care. My daughter has carried on the tradition, not with woodworking, but by planning ahead to get inexpensive but meaningful gifts for people on special occasions. There is often an inside joke connected to the gift or simply something that says, "I noticed how much you like this."

Traditions can add a level of romance to special occasions. I have a friend who rememorizes his wedding vows every anniversary and, at precisely 6:00 p.m. (the hour they got married), he recites them to his wife. You can imagine how this makes her feel. I could see the sparkle in her eyes as she watched him tell me about this special tradition.

Making sure you have special events on the calendar is important for keeping joy in your marriage. Special events give you something to anticipate as you plan together, they give you time away where the focus is only on your relationship, and they give you memories to share for years to come. Depending on the budget, some couples go camping, some go to exotic destinations. No matter what, get creative, and you can find something that will bring you both joy on any budget.

RELATIONAL SEX

One of our goals in this book is to help you rekindle the unique and pleasurable joy-bonding that only happens with sex. As you might expect, given what we have said about the left brain and the right brain, there is a vast difference in your sexual experience if you are participating with your relational engine engaged, or if you are simply executing a task with your relational circuits off.

As with other types of play, it is a great idea to plan ahead for times of sex. Knowing it is coming can add joyful anticipation. It is also good to be spontaneous at times. Putting sex in the category of "play" and thinking of the goal as "joy" helps keep the experience relational and satisfying for both partners.

I have some good friends who simply call their bed "the playground." Both the husband and the wife grew up in dysfunctional homes. When they got married, they decided to start a new heritage for their children and prioritize intimacy in their marriage at a level that had not been modeled by their parents. That commitment to intimacy included planning for sex. Since they both work and the husband is frequently away on business, one of the ways they keep their love life fresh is by leaving each other notes throughout the week that say, for example,

"ETN: 2/8." It means "Estimated Time to Nakedness: 2 days 8 hours." When both parties are leaving notes like this around the house, it is hard not to see one and smile. Preparation builds the anticipation and helps make sex romantic and not just a task or duty. I also have friends who keep track of how many states and countries they have had sex in. Not long ago, they confided that they had covered all fifty states and twenty-seven countries. More than once, they added a day to a trip or drove across a state line just to check another state or country off their list. Now that is planning ahead! This same friend recently told me, "I can't imagine a life in which marriage isn't your highest priority. We have made it a point to play together regularly, and sex is a big part of that."

For some couples, relational sex is no problem, but for many, sex in marriage is a big problem. There can be several reasons for this, and the root issues can get complicated. Often there is sexual trauma in one of the partners. Sometimes fear, anger, resentment, and a lack of attachment drive the issue. A lack of desire for sex in marriage can create a lot of questions like, "Is my partner cheating on me? Is my partner more interested in a same-sex relationship? Am I doing something wrong?"

Another source of damage to enjoyable, relational sex in marriage is related to the damage caused by pornography and extramarital affairs. Both of these can have profound effects on a couple's sex life. Pornography, among its many dangers, turns sex into a performance rather than a bonding experience. I have talked to several women who feel dirty after sex with their husbands because they are basically recreating pornographic videos he has seen. Some couples watch porn together as if it will help their sex lives, but porn doesn't promote relational sex. It promotes sex as performance in which people focus on themselves and their own fulfillment rather than something mutual. It also tears down trust and intimacy by moving the focus away from loving and pleasing the other person.

Here are some tips on ways to keep your sexual play time relationally joyful rather than fear-based and mechanical:

- Spend some time naked together before you start.
- Share appreciation about the other person or remember happy times together while looking into their eyes (refer back to the "A" in CAKE in chapter 2).
- Touch one another, start to engage, then stop and take some more time to cuddle.
- Help each other have a great experience.
- Rest and cuddle before you end your time together.

Here are a few don'ts:

- Don't talk about problems or tasks that need to be done.

- Don't talk about the kids.
- Don't be afraid to give guidance or make suggestions.
- Don't simply roll over or disappear after you are done. Take some time to stay connected.

Making times of sexual intimacy fun for both and relationally bonding will keep it from turning into a task to be completed in a nonrelational, nonjoyful way.

SOCIAL ROUTINES

I met a couple whose marriage almost ended after twenty years together. It was a shock to everyone who knew them because they were active in Christian ministry and seemed to have a model marriage. But years of prioritizing work and kids over marriage had taken its toll. They felt like strangers. They resented each other. Both placed the blame solidly on the other for their problems. They saw no path forward and were ready to throw in the towel.

Today, this couple leads a nonprofit helping people whose marriages have been damaged by years of neglect. What is their secret? They made two major changes in their lives. First, they changed the way they communicated. When a problem arose, they first prayed about it, then journaled about it, then wrote an email to their spouse about it. Only after all these steps did they talk

> *Ending the day happy to be together is a huge part of building a social routine of playing together.*

about it. To help them build time for communication into their marriage, they bought a dog so they had a reason to go for a walk in the park every night and talk. The second change they made was to create a social routine of playing together.

Taking a daily walk together was a start. They also established a weekly date night, began scheduling get-away weekends every few months, and developed a pattern for ending the day happy to be together.[1]

Ending the day happy to be together is a huge part of building a social routine of playing together. This starts by establishing two rules for the end of the day.

Rule #1: We will stop talking about problems and tasks thirty minutes before we go to bed.

Rule #2: We will play together and share appreciation before we turn off the lights.

It is amazing how much difference it can make to follow these two simple rules. Far too many couples go to bed talking about problems and planning for tasks, then wonder why they sleep so poorly and live with so much stress in their marriage.

SHRINKING THE GAP

Friendship is the foundation of a great marriage. One of the keys to a great friendship is playing together and having fun. When we stop having fun in our marriage, a lot of other problems start to look bigger. However, playing together can keep our joy high and our friendship strong.

In our exercise section, Chris will provide you with lots of ideas for ways you can play together. These exercises will include planning special events, practicing relational sex, and a variety of activities to help you spend more time playing in your marriage. Don't forget to see the additional exercises in Appendix 1.

EXERCISES FOR HABIT #1: PLAYING TOGETHER

Think about this: If you are going swimming, are you the kind of person who cautiously steps into the pool by slowly dipping your toes into the water, then placing your feet, ankles, and body into the pool? Or are you someone who simply runs to the edge and fearlessly leaps with a big cannonball splash?

Regardless of your preference, the following exercises will work for any personality—whether your approach to life is bold or more cautious—so have fun and get connected. However, don't force it. If one of you needs to stop or rest, please honor that request. Play stays fun when we are tender toward weaknesses and we respect limitations. It is important to learn how to let the other person know when you are getting overwhelmed by something and need to pause or stop. Some couples have code words, like "avocado" (I made that one up). But the point is to have signals that keep interactions safe and enjoyable by letting the other person know when you need a break.

Earlier in the book we mentioned the hormone **oxytocin**. Let's take a closer look at this important chemical. Oxytocin is sometimes called "the bonding hormone." When it is present, it *personalizes joy* by telling our brain that *our spouse* is the source of the good stuff. It is like glue that helps us stay attached. Oxytocin makes us feel generous, trusting, and connected with the one we love. This love hormone increases with skin-to-skin contact, so you will notice each exercise includes a variety of ways to physically connect. The exercises may look modest—even rigid—at first glance, but watch the sparks fly when you intentionally interact with the one you love!

How well the exercises go for you comes down to one main factor: the status of your brain's relational circuits.[2] If your relational brain is awake and alert, you will be able to start some joy. If your relational brain is asleep, the exercises will feel tedious and tiresome. For this reason, each exercise includes steps to activate your relational brain so you get the most out of each interaction. Pausing to feel thankful will warm up your relational brain, so anytime you feel disconnected during an exercise, this step will reboot your relational circuits for maximum joy. And, while the exercises are designed for you to practice in a sequential order, you and your beloved can practice exercises as often as you like and in the order that works best for you. Go, strap on your seat belt and enjoy the ride!

Practice eye smiles ⏱ 15 MIN

1. Looking at your spouse is one of the best ways for your brain to build joy while voice tone is a close second. This means seeing your spouse and hearing your spouse's voice can be invigorating—as long as joy is the emotion you are amplifying! The muscles around the eyes are where spontaneous joy shows up, not the mouth. **Eye smiles** are what happen when we are glad to be together and our eyes "light up" seeing the one we love.

   Eye smiles engage the brain's joy center and nonverbal communication happens at a rapid rate, so you want to 1) start out feeling relational when you begin this exercise, and 2) look away for rest at the right times when you feel like you are no longer growing joy. Don't force it! This interaction is meant to be an interactive joy and rest sequence, not a stare-down contest. As soon as you feel the joy is no longer growing by looking at your spouse, it is time to look away for a few seconds and disengage to rest. Rest is a normal response, so be sure to rest as needed. Return to the eye smiles as soon as you feel ready and it looks like your partner is ready.

Joy can bring up a variety of reactions, so don't be surprised if different emotions come up while you practice, from tears to laughter. If this exercise is uncomfortable for you, you may want to experiment with playing music in the background as you practice this skill. Try both high-energy and low-energy music to see what you prefer.

NOTE: Try this exercise several times in different ways and see which methods connect with you the best—a little practice goes a long way!

2. While cuddling, reminisce about one of your favorite memories with your spouse. ⏱ 5 MIN

3. Next, play some music you both enjoy, then sit across from each other knee to knee while you hold hands. Without using words, look into each other's eyes with a warm smile (connect), then look away (rest) and take a breather whenever you need one. The goal here is to connect, then rest again and again for two minutes. ⏱ 2 MIN

4. When finished, hold hands or cuddle while you discuss how this exercise felt for you. What did you notice? ⏱ **3 MIN**

5. Close with several minutes of quiet cuddling and resting together. ⏱ **5 MIN**

Date Night ⏱ **15 MIN**

1. Plan a special date night doing something fun you both enjoy. As part of your evening, be sure to include the following exercise:
   Reminisce some of the highlights from your wedding day and honeymoon. What do you remember about your special day that made you smile? Try to come up with as many fun moments as you can remember. ⏱ **7 MIN**
   NOTE: *If for some reason your wedding day does not invoke fun feelings, then think about a vacation together or another memory that is meaningful for both of you.*

2. At the end of your time, hold hands or cuddle, then share what was fun about this special outing. Highlight three things you enjoy about your partner's heart and character. ⏱ **5 MIN**
   Close with several minutes of quiet cuddling and resting together. ⏱ **3 MIN**

Get Relational ⏱ 15 MIN

1. While holding hands or cuddling, spend several minutes telling each other the qualities you enjoy about your partner. Be sure to look into your lover's eyes and try to include moments you observed these qualities in action. ⏱ 5 MIN
   EXAMPLE: *I really like how generous and thoughtful you are. Just today you surprised me with my favorite bag of coffee beans that you know I love!*

2. Notice how you feel when giving and receiving appreciation. Talk about what you notice as you practiced the previous step. ⏱ 3 MIN

3. Take some time kissing like you did when you were first married. ⏱ 2 MIN
   HINT: *You may want to brush your teeth first if you had onions or garlic for lunch.*

4. Close with several minutes of quiet cuddling and resting together. ⏱ 5 MIN

Just between Us ⏱ 15 MIN

1. You will want some privacy for this exercise. (You can wear your birthday suit if you like.) While lying in bed holding each other, start by sharing some highlights from your day. ⏱ 3 MIN
   NOTE: *Avoid talking about anything upsetting.*

2. Spend some time caressing each other while you share stories about your favorite intimate moments together. Include specifics about what made these times meaningful for you.
⏱ 3 MIN

3. Next, take some time to cuddle and quiet without caressing while you both place a hand on your partner's chest to feel his or her heartbeat.
⏱ 3 MIN

4. Now, continue the caressing for another several minutes followed by cuddling while you take turns listening to each other's heartbeat. ⏱ 3 MIN Then enjoy some relational sexual intimacy that brings you both smiles and satisfaction. (Take as much time as you need for this step!)

5. Have some time to rest, then close by expressing appreciation to your spouse about what you enjoy about his/her heart, mind, and body.
⏱ 3 MIN

CHAPTER 5

Habit #2: Listen for Emotion

I HAVE LED DOZENS of marriage retreats and always ask the couples, "What are the top three problems in marriage?" The number one answer at almost every retreat is "communication." Most of us had it drilled into our thinking that communication is the key to a good marriage, and there is a lot of truth to this. We are going to address the issue of communication in this chapter. However, we are going to start with why communication isn't always the first step in dealing with our problems.

PRINCIPLE 1: COMMUNICATION IS USELESS (AND SOMETIMES DANGEROUS) IF YOUR RELATIONAL CIRCUITS AREN'T ON.

Marriage specialist Gary Smalley developed one of the most watched self-help videos in history called *Keys to*

Loving Relationships.[1] In one of his sessions, he describes what it is like to try to communicate with someone who is shut down or, using the brain science imagery from chapter 2, someone whose switch is off. He uses a fist to illustrate the problem. Imagine your partner's shut-down relational circuits as a fist. Because your partner's switch is off, he or she has gone into full self-protection mode and has stopped talking. Now imagine your other hand flapping like it is talking to your fist. (Go ahead, try it.) Trying to talk to someone whose switch is off is like trying to talk to a fist. The words just bounce off. There is not really any communication taking place.

The idea of your open hand trying to talk to your fist is a good picture of one person trying to talk to another person who is emotionally shut down. That person isn't really listening, because their switch is off. When this happens, your words just bounce off the hardened emotional shell created by their shut-down relational circuits.

One of the reasons people shut down and quit talking is to protect others from what they feel like saying. If you poke at them until they talk, you may not like what comes out. Another reason people shut down is to protect themselves. They are afraid that anything they say "can and will be used against them." Shutting down always happens because the switch in our brain has flipped off.

Brenda and I know all too well what this is like. Early in our marriage, I noticed that when I got triggered, the relational circuitry in my brain shut down. I didn't yell at Brenda. I just stopped talking altogether. She didn't know what to do with me when that happened. At that point, the only tool in her marriage kit was communication. So she would do her best to get me to talk. The problem was when I was triggered and my relational brain shut down, talking was not a very good idea.

Years later—it felt like a lifetime—we started learning some of the brain science behind good communication. Brenda tried something different one day. We had been arguing, and I had shut down. I simply wasn't talking at all. Brenda was sitting on the bed and I was sitting on a couch. Normally, she would have tried to get me to talk, but this time she looked at me and realized that my brain's relational circuits were totally shut down and that talking wouldn't do any good if they didn't come back on.

Instead of pushing the conversation, she said, "Do you mind if I come sit next to you?" That caught me totally off guard. My defenses were up and ready to repel a barrage of words. I had no defense in place for someone who wanted to be with me when I wasn't at my best. Once she sat next to me, she asked, "Is it okay if I hold your hand?" I looked at her like she was from another planet. "You aren't very good at this fighting thing, are you?" I asked. But I let her hold my hand, and I could feel something change inside. It was like a lock sprang open and my relational circuits came back online. Suddenly, being in relationship with

Brenda felt more important than winning the argument.

Brenda was modeling for me what it looked like to keep the relationship bigger than the problem. Since then, we have tried to make that our "go-to phrase" when we get upset. It is not uncommon for one of us to say, "Let's keep the relationship bigger than the problem." This is the clue that we need to get our relational circuits on before we continue our conversation.

> *Sometimes we fail to communicate because we are trying to communicate with someone who is totally shut down.*

Brenda jumpstarted my relational engine before trying to communicate. This is exactly what Gary Smalley had recommended in his talk. He had said that before you try to talk to someone who is shut down, you need to help them open up. The fist needs to relax so the hand can open and receive what is being said. To illustrate this point, he took the hand that was doing the talking and had it begin to stroke the fist in a comforting way that allowed it to relax. Once that happened, communication came easily.

Sometimes we don't fail to communicate because we aren't trying. It is because we are trying to communicate with someone who is totally shut down.

PRINCIPLE #2: LISTEN FOR EMOTIONS
BEFORE TRYING TO SOLVE PROBLEMS

Your brain processes data from right to left. This means the relational right side of your brain gets data before it goes to the problem-solving left side of your brain. In the same way, communication needs to start on the right side of your brain by listening for emotions *before* sending the information to the left side and trying to solve the problems you hear. This process is called validation. It is the most important tool I know for keeping relationships bigger than problems. You validate someone's emotions by accurately identifying what they are feeling and offer some explanation that shows you understand why the person is feeling that way.

Validating doesn't mean agreeing with what someone is feeling. You don't have to agree that they should be feeling a certain way. You simply need to acknowledge that they are, in fact, feeling that way. For example, if my son comes into the room afraid of a storm, I don't have to say, "You are right to be afraid of the storm," in order to validate his emotion. I can say, "The loud thunder and strong wind can be kind of scary, can't they?" My goal is to get my son to nod his head in agreement. Once I get agreement that I have understood his emotion, I can move to problem-solving by asking, "Would you like to stay in here with mom and dad?"

The brain science behind validation is pretty straightforward. The problem-solving part of your brain tends to listen for problems. The relational part of your brain listens for emotions. If your relational circuits are off, you will find it almost impossible to listen for emotions. All you will want to do is listen for problems that you can fix.

I had a couple come to see me for premarital counseling, and I tried an exercise to help them understand the importance of listening for emotions. First, I asked them if there was a problem in their life they had trouble agreeing on how to fix. They looked at each other immediately, as if to say, "We know what that is." The man was convinced it was better to build a house before getting married. His fiancée wasn't quite so sure. I said, "Why don't you guys discuss this problem while you have a third party present, and it will give me a chance to see how you go about problem-solving." Well, it wasn't pretty. Before this conversation, they looked like the typical young couple in love, excited about the upcoming wedding. Within a few minutes, they had pulled away from each other and the conversation was becoming rather tense. I decided I had had enough fun at their expense and it was time to intervene.

"Let's try this again," I suggested. "Only this time, I don't want you to listen for the problem. I only want you to listen for the *emotion* the other person is expressing. Name that emotion accurately and give a sense of how big it is for them." I then had the young man listen as his fiancée shared why she didn't think it was a good idea to build the house before the wedding. Anyone watching this conversation would have easily caught that the emotion she was feeling was anxiety. She was afraid that the house would become his focus and that the wedding would be an afterthought. Confident that this was a fairly straightforward answer, I asked the young man, "What emotion did you hear?" He said, "Anger." That caught me off guard. "Really?" I asked, then said, "You are either very intuitive or a really bad listener." He said, "I think I am really intuitive." "Okay," I responded, "tell me where you heard anger." Without hesitating, he said, "She's angry because she knows she is losing this argument."

I suggested we try the exercise again, and this time, rather than being intuitive, he try to repeat back to her the emotion *she* thought she was feeling. This time, he hit a home run. He said, "She's afraid that if we build the house before the wedding that I will get so caught up in the details of the project, I won't be emotionally available to her on one of the biggest days of her life." She started to cry. He got it. She felt understood, and feeling understood made her feel safe. She suddenly blurted out, "Go ahead and build the house!" That caught me off guard, too. It also showed me that she trusted him. However, I made them slow down and said it was her turn to practice listening for emotions. I wanted him to share with her why it was so important to him that the house get built first. His initial response was that there was nothing emotional about the decision, it was just logical. I nodded. "We'll see."

The young lady had to ask a few probing questions, but eventually he realized how much he wanted his dad to be proud of him. "If I had a house built for my family before I got married, my dad would be so proud of me." Saying this out loud touched something deep inside and soon both of them were in tears. The simple exercise of listening for emotions rather than problems had brought them back together at a deeper level than before and helped them resolve their problem without sacrificing the relationship.

Counterfeit Validation

There is a counterfeit form of validation that doesn't work at all. Instead of validating the other person's emotions accurately, we simply say, "I understand." This is counterfeit validation. When you say, "I understand," instead of taking the time to actually name your partner's emotion correctly, what the other person hears is, "Shut up! I'm tired of listening." Adding the words "Sweetie" or "Honey" or "Dear" doesn't help. It just makes the statement feel even more condescending. However, you can say, "I understand this is making you feel scared or angry" because you are naming the emotion accurately. But left to themselves, the words "I understand" tend to shut down conversation rather than validate emotion.

SAD-SAD: Six Core Negative Emotions

To help you listen for emotion, we want to introduce you to six core negative emotions. These six are often combined to form other negative emotions (such as dread, which is most commonly a combination of fear and despair), but if you understand these six and learn to listen for them, your ability to validate emotions accurately should skyrocket.

We call these negative emotions the "SAD-SAD" emotions because SAD-SAD helps you remember what they are. Since the brain runs best on joy, these emotions all represent some way in which joy is stopped, stalled, or robbed. Each of these emotions also affects your body in some specific ways, which is helpful when you are trying to recognize your own emotions or those of someone else.

SADNESS. "I have lost something that brought me joy." Sadness is a low-energy emotion. It feels like someone stepped on the brakes, and your body has lost some of its drive. Sadness can show itself as a pouty lip, tears in the eyes, or sagging posture. Whenever there are changes in relationships and routines, a sense of loss can create sadness. Perhaps your spouse is unavailable when you want to connect, or you schedule a date night and have to cancel it. Noticing the physical cues can help you recognize that your partner is sad. Validating the emotions can help your spouse feel like you are sharing the burden rather than leaving him/her alone in disappointment and loss.

ANXIETY. "I fear not being able to find joy as I look

at the future." Whereas sadness is a low-energy emotion, anxiety is high energy. It triggers our fight, flight, or freeze response, which shoots adrenaline all through our body.

Fear and anxiety go hand in hand. Fear is the emotional response to what threatens me while anxiety is rooted in imagination. We can all imagine scenarios we know would be overwhelming to us; therefore, everyone feels anxiety at times. Staying connected with people and knowing that I am not alone helps disarm anxiety. Validating your partner's anxious emotions can help them feel connected and secure.

DESPAIR. "I feel like joy is impossible." Despair is another low-energy emotion. It can suck the life out of your body so that you have no energy and don't feel like doing anything. It can make your arms and hands hang limp. When you look at the future and see no hope of joy, you will feel despair. Despair means you do not have the time or the resources to fix a problem that is stealing your joy. Despair is hopelessness and is found at the root of most depression. It is the feeling that there is no solution for your problems. Despair can be hard to validate for some people because they want to give the other person some hope and help fix things rather than simply being present and happy to be with them even in their despair. We need to validate first and make sure the other person knows we see what they are going through before we jump to comforting them.

SHAME. "I feel like hiding because I can tell I don't bring you joy." Shame is also a low-energy emotion. You feel like hanging your head because you don't expect someone to be happy to see you. You want to justify yourself so you don't feel like it is your fault that another person doesn't want to be with you. Healthy shame is recognizing changes that need to be made to your attitudes and behaviors. However, toxic shame is believing that you are simply a bad person and that your very presence is a cause for shame. Validating the emotion of shame in others can help people understand that you are happy to be with them even when they don't expect it.

ANGER. "I want something to stop right now because it is robbing me of joy and causing me pain." Anger is a high-energy emotion. It also triggers adrenaline as your body gears itself up for a fight or to make a situation stop. Anger tends to be motivated by the desire to stop pain or establish justice. When you want to cause someone else pain, it is often because you feel wronged and want them to feel the pain you feel. It can be hard to validate anger when it is directed at you, but it can also help to defuse situations that have escalated to say something like, "You are angry at me because you feel betrayed, like I am putting my own needs ahead of yours." Validating anger may lead you to own the truth of what is going on, but, at the very least, it will show that you understand their feelings.

DISGUST. "I feel like recoiling from a person or situation." Disgust is a low-energy emotion often connected with the desire to vomit. It relates to your body's protective instinct to get rid of poison you may eat accidentally. Disgust makes you want to get as far away from something (or someone) as you can. One of the experiences that helped me understand disgust was learning to change diapers. It takes a certain amount of maturity to be able to feel disgust at the odor and texture of what you are dealing with and still be happy to be with your baby and do the needed task. Validating disgust is important because it lets people know that someone is willing to share their displeasure and stay relationally connected.

Your Brain and Listening for Emotions

Becoming an expert at listening for emotions is the first step toward becoming an expert at keeping relationships bigger than problems. When you listen for emotions, you force your relational right brain to stay engaged. This keeps your relational circuits on. When you don't listen for emotions, but focus on problems instead, it tends to shut down your relational right brain and keep you stuck in your problem-solving left brain.

I can tell when I shift into the problem-solving part of my brain because I either interrupt or I stop listening once I hear the problem. If I don't catch myself, I will respond condescendingly to my wife's problem, only to find out that I stopped listening too soon and addressed the wrong problem. If I don't apologize for my lack of relational connection and start listening for her emotions, the situation tends to escalate. This is because I am fully in nonrelational, problem-solving mode where winning is more important than relating.

> *Winning rarely strengthens the relationship.*

Of course, the problem with winning these conversations is that winning rarely strengthens the relationship. The more often you find a way to win even when you are wrong, the more twisted your character becomes. To put this in perspective, in extreme cases we call people who have lost their conscience and only care about winning sociopaths. They don't care who they hurt as long as they win. I trust most of us aren't sociopaths, but that doesn't mean that we can't—from time to time—adopt sociopathic behavior that stops caring about how the relationship is affected and just wants to be right.

SHRINKING THE GAP

As we saw at the beginning of this chapter, brain science teaches us that right brain activity needs to come before left-brain activity. This means that validation (a right-brain activity) must come before comforting (the left-brain action of making a problem smaller and thus more manageable). The order is crucial. Right-brain activity has to precede left-brain activity or the whole process will create even more problems. In our book *Rare Leadership*, Jim Wilder and I present a simple acronym for remembering the order this process needs to take: VCR. Validate, Comfort, Repattern.

VALIDATION. The right brain *validates* by accurately naming the emotion the other person is feeling and accurately identifying how big it is for them. In order to do this, we need to become skilled at listening for emotions, which is what this chapter is all about.

COMFORT. After your right brain validates, your left brain *comforts* by problem-solving with the person. The goal is to offer strategies and perspectives that make the person's problems smaller and thus more manageable. Comfort includes finding something to appreciate and feel thankful for—even in the midst of the emotion.

REPATTERNING. As we experience the process of validating and comforting again and again, our brain learns to make that pattern its new normal. The VCR pattern becomes our natural habit for responding to our own emotions as well as to those of others around us. In time, you stop being afraid of those emotions, because your brain learns that it can recover from them.

Until your brain learns this new pattern, it will tend to avoid people and situations that generate feelings it doesn't know how to handle. If you can't recover from anger, you will avoid people and situations that trigger anger. If you can't return to joy from fear, you will avoid people and situations that trigger fear. However, as your brain learns how it can return to joy through validation and comfort, those emotions become less overwhelming and you are able to stay relational and engaged in situations that used to trigger you.

People who skip validation and go straight to left-brain comforting generally make the situation worse. We call these people "fixers." They are more interested in fixing you than listening to your emotions. The point here is that both validation and comfort are important, but the order is even more important. It is great to help people make their problems smaller and more manageable, but we *first* have to listen for and validate their emotions. If you get the order wrong, the person will feel like you don't care.

In this week's exercises, Chris will give you a variety of scenarios to help you turn on your relational circuits and practice listening for and accurately naming emotions. We want to focus on mild emotions first. Just like any other skill, you need to practice on a "beginner level" before advancing.

EXERCISES FOR HABIT #2: LISTEN FOR EMOTION

Welcome to the second round of exercises. In this section, you and your spouse train your brain's ability to perceive, read, and listen for emotions. With practice, you can learn to activate your relational circuits so you keep relationships bigger than emotions, pain, and problems. A big part of training the relational brain to listen for emotions involves a skill known as **mindsight,** which you can think of as your relationship reader. You use mindsight to "read" and interpret the other person's body language, voice tone, and facial expressions. When mindsight is accurate, you see and understand the mind and heart of your partner. For example, when you say, "You look tired. Do you need to rest?" your spouse feels seen and understood. This skill creates intimacy, connection, and much-needed resilience to help process negative emotions.

When mindsight is faulty or "leaky," then unprocessed pain from our past leaks into the present, which disrupts our ability to see, hear, and understand our partner.[2] One spouse may overreact from a word, voice tone, or behavior that reminds him/her of something painful from the past. At this point, we no longer clearly gauge what is happening inside our partner's mind, so we misread what is said and misunderstand our partner. This broken "relationship reader" creates pain and leads to conflict and miscommunication.

This heartache is avoidable! One way we can correct this unhelpful pattern is to share nonverbal stories where we must rely on our emotional brain to "read" our partner and then predict how he or she will respond to better help our partner understand what we are trying to convey.

The following exercises aim to enhance our brain's relationship reader. Our body is the canvas for our emotional brain. Like a work of art, our body tells a story about our emotional well-being. Paying attention to our muscle tension and breathing can tell us if big emotions are present or even sneaking up on us. We will practice the one-two punch of validation and comfort to repattern our brain to better read emotions.

Happy and Sad ⏱ 15 MIN

1. While holding hands, share three things from your day that made you happy, then highlight one thing that made you sad. Include how your body felt in the happy and the sad. ⏱ 3 MIN
    For example, *I was glad when my coworker helped me on a project and this felt refreshing and "lighter" in my body.*

2. Next, your partner will express the emotional content from what you said, including his/her observations. (You can take one item at a time if this works better.) ⏱ 3 MIN
    HAPPY EXAMPLE: *When you were glad your coworker helped you today, this felt refreshing and you felt lighter. I even noticed a smile appear on your face while you were sharing.*

SAD EXAMPLE: *When you observed the person yelling at her young daughter in the grocery store today, you felt very unhappy and your body felt heavy. I noticed your energy level dropped and your tone of voice sounded sad while you were telling me this story.*

3. Switch roles. ⏱ **6 MIN**

4. Discuss how you feel after practicing this exercise, then close with quiet cuddling and resting together. ⏱ **3 MIN**

Joy Reminiscing ⏱ 15 MIN

1. Think of a joyful memory with your spouse from the previous year. ⏱ **2 MIN**

2. Before telling your story, write a few notes on the following details: ⏱ **1 MIN**
   My body: *What was I feeling in my body?*
   My emotions: *What emotions were present?*

3. While holding hands and gazing into each other's eyes, briefly tell your stories and include the above details. ⏱ **6 MIN**

4. When finished, take turns highlighting and validating the emotional content from the story your partner shared. ⏱ **3 MIN**
   EXAMPLE: *Our weekend getaway to the beach was a special time for you as you were feeling encouraged. Our time together helped you rest*

and relax so your body felt peaceful and your shoulders were no longer tense.

5. Discuss what you noticed from this exercise, then close with quiet cuddling and resting together. ⏱ **3 MIN**

Mirroring My Mate ⏱ **15 MIN**

1. Think about a moment from your day when you felt peaceful, then think of another moment when peace was absent. These examples should be short and simple. ⏱ **2 MIN**

2. Once you have two examples in mind, briefly review:

   My body: *What was my body feeling?*
   My emotions: *What emotions were present?*
   ⏱ **2 MIN**

   Here are two examples:

   Peace: *While enjoying my cup of coffee this morning, I felt joyful, calm, and peaceful.*
   No Peace: *Driving to work, I was stuck in traffic. At that point I felt anxious and restless; my stomach twisted into tight knots.*

3. Now, take turns telling your stories including body sensations and emotions. Listener, once your spouse finishes telling one story, tell the story back to him or her nonverbally (using your body gestures, facial expressions and

acting-out movements) based on what you observed and heard. Do this for both stories. (This step improves mindsight.) ⏱ **8 MIN**

REMINDER: *The elements of a nonverbal story include eye contact, facial expressions, vocal expressions, posture, gestures, timing, and intensity.*

4. When you both finish your stories, discuss what you noticed from this exercise, then close with some quiet cuddling and resting together. ⏱ **3 MIN**

A Few of My Favorite Things ⏱ 15 MIN

1. Take turns sharing a *favorite activity* you enjoyed growing up. Include reasons why this activity was so meaningful for you and a special memory associated with this activity. ⏱ **3 MIN**

   EXAMPLE: *I used to ride my bicycle all around my neighborhood and this was special for me because I would enjoy the wind on my face. I remember having my paper route and how fun it was to deliver newspapers . . .*

2. After each person shares his or her *favorite activity*, take turns validating each other and highlight how important this was to him or her. ⏱ **2 MIN**

   EXAMPLE: *I can tell you really enjoyed riding your bike when you were younger and delivering*

newspapers. Feeling the wind on your face was
very freeing for you . . .

3. Now take turns sharing your *favorite food* along
   with reasons why this food is a favorite. Include
   a special memory associated with this food.
   ⏱ 3 MIN

4. After each person shares his or her favorite
   food, take turns validating each other and highlight how important this food is to him or her.
   ⏱ 2 MIN

5. Next, take turns sharing one of your favorite
   songs. Include why this song is important to
   you and any special memories associated with
   this song. ⏱ 3 MIN
   NOTE: *You can insert a favorite movie, book, or*
   Scripture verse here instead of a song if you like.

6. After each person shares his or her favorite
   song, validate emotions and highlight how important this song is for him or her. ⏱ 1 MIN

7. Close with a moment of quiet cuddling and
   resting together. ⏱ 1 MIN

You will find no shortage of opportunities to listen for
emotions in your interactions with the one you love. God
created us with emotions because, simply, we are made in
God's image, and God has emotions! Emotions are not
bad; they are signals alerting us that something needs

to be addressed. Marcus and I want to encourage you to continue the validation and comfort with your spouse as opportunities arise. Practice happy and sad on a daily basis, and watch what happens with your joy levels! The dinner hour tends to be an ideal window to practice this exercise, as you can review your day and connect with your loved ones. Sharpen your brain's ability to notice and listen for emotions by expressing what was satisfying from your day as well as noticing and expressing what was not satisfying. Your brain and your marriage bond will thank you!

CHAPTER 6

Habit #3: Appreciate Daily

IN SOME WAYS, marriage isn't that complicated. When appreciation levels are high, your marriage is joy-filled. When resentment replaces appreciation, marriage feels like a burden. This is because the two most powerful forces for building joy or missing out on joy are appreciation and resentment. Appreciation attracts. Resentment repels. To put this in brain science terms, appreciation builds joy bonds and resentment builds fear bonds. Appreciation is also a great way to fill up the joy bucket, which grows our emotional capacity.

More and more studies are demonstrating the power of appreciation. One study done at Indiana University began with 43 people who were engaged in counseling for anxiety or depression.[1] Of these participants, 22 were assigned "gratitude intervention" while the rest simply

> *When appreciation is lacking, the joy gap tends to grow, and as it grows, it tends to fill with resentment.*

continued to attend their normal therapy sessions without doing the gratitude exercises.[2] Those who participated in the gratitude activities showed "profound" and "long-lasting" improvement beyond that of the participants who simply went to counseling.

When appreciation is high, joy is easy. When appreciation is low, resentment takes over, and you start looking for ways to avoid each other instead of ways to spend more time together. We started this book by talking about the need to shrink the joy gap in our marriages. One of the best ways to shrink the joy gap is appreciation. However, when appreciation is lacking, the joy gap tends to grow and, as it grows, it tends to fill with resentment.

GRATITUDE VS. APPRECIATION

I used to think I was pretty good at appreciation. After all, my mom did a good job of teaching me to say "please" and "thank you." So I told my wife "thank you" quite a bit. However, I have learned there is a big difference between saying "thank you" and feeling appreciation. The former is a left-brain task that does little, if anything, to bond people together. The latter is a right-brain experience that bonds people in joy. Taking time to dwell on what I appreciate about my wife is a much different experience than simply saying "thank you" for something she does.

Appreciation is a feeling of shared joy. Even when it seems like you are alone and feeling joy, there is usually a relational component to the emotion. Thus, when you look at a sunset or stand quietly in a park for a few minutes, letting the beauty and sensation of the moment sink in, you are experiencing appreciation. You may feel like you are all alone, but really it is a shared experience because it is activating the relational part of your brain. For some, it is a shared experience with the Creator. For others, it reminds them of people they love and fuels a desire to share the moment with them—either wishing they were there or anticipating telling them about it. I think this is one of the reasons posting pictures of food, cats, nature, and kids is so popular. We post pictures online because we sense that our joy will be more complete if we can share our experience with someone else.

When I first started being intentional about building the habit of appreciation, I struggled with anxiety. I discovered that anxiety can make it pretty hard to stay in appreciation mode. The first time I intentionally decided to spend five minutes in a state of appreciation, my experience went something like this. I grabbed my favorite coffee mug and prepared my favorite blend of cream, sugar, and coffee (probably in that order), then held the mug in my hands and breathed in the aroma. I had just started to enjoy the moment when my left brain chimed in and said, "This is the stupidest thing you've ever done!" Instead of helping me quiet my anxious thoughts, I became more agitated. I am so left-brain dominant that my ability to actually appreciate what I was experiencing was easily sabotaged. Because I hadn't been practicing appreciation as a normal part of my life, it was nearly impossible to flip the switch and engage my right brain just by choice. I learned that it can take weeks of intentional practice to build joy through a routine of focused appreciation.

ESTABLISHING A ROUTINE

Appreciation is often the hidden ingredient that determines if a marriage is strong or weak, admirable or anemic. The brain that is trained on appreciation will scan the environment for good things while the untrained brain becomes critical and all too quick to find fault in other people.

Practice feeling and sharing appreciation as often as you can. You will notice the benefits from the moment you wake up in the morning to the time your head hits the pillow at night. Add some rest into the equation by not only practicing the exercises in this section, but also trying to maintain a steady diet of the following activities:

- Verbalize the qualities you enjoy about your spouse.
- Continue to hug, cuddle, and kiss like you mean it.

- Let your face light up when you see your spouse. Use your voice to convey the love you feel for your beloved.
- Take a hot bath or a shower together. Use your words and touch to express how much you enjoy the one you love.

Remembering What You Appreciate

One great way to build the habit of appreciation in your marriage is to put it in writing. It is life-giving for both of you to spend time remembering what you appreciate about your husband or wife. The practice of putting things in writing slows you down and lets you dwell on the reasons for appreciation and the feelings that appreciation brings.

Letters. One week when Brenda was out of town for several days, I found it hard to fall asleep. I decided to write her a letter. In the letter, I wrote out some of the things I appreciated about her. The letter went something like this.

> I know I can be distant and make you feel unappreciated, but really, nearly every good thing in my life today has its roots in you. You are the adventurous one. You planned surprise birthday vacations for me, you made sure we had extended family trips in the mountains, you always find

ways to make the home more beautiful. I tend to complain about the money and rob some of the joy by focusing on the cost. But as I sit here alone, missing you, I realize how much richness you add to my life. My best memories all involve you. Your passion for life and willingness to spend something to make those memories has made our lives better.

Writing a letter like this now and then can help you remember what there is to appreciate about the person you married. Just remembering that you appreciate someone and dwelling on that appreciation strengthens the bond between you.

Lists. Another way that writing can help with appreciation is to make lists. Then over a period of time, write blogs or journal style entries about the items on your list. For example, make a top five list of character qualities you appreciate, then find a story that embodies each quality and write about it. Here are some other top five lists to consider:

- Vacation memories
- Holiday memories
- Memories of realizing you were falling in love
- Romantic memories after the honeymoon
- Joyful parenting memories

Five categories of joyful memories with five stories in each category will give you *twenty-five* joyful memories to fuel your appreciation of the other person. Write these out, give them titles, and keep them handy so that when you are struggling to remember what you appreciate about your spouse, you can pull out the lists and spend some time remembering what you appreciate. It is a good idea to make lists when you feel connected and relational. These lists then become tools you can refer to in order to help regain perspective when you do get upset.

SHRINKING THE GAP

I (Chris) can still remember how hard it was for my wife, Jen, to rest and calm down when she needed a breather. Jen was the first to say she had a busy mind. "Busy" was an understatement.

If my wife's mind was a car, she would be a Lamborghini or a Maserati, speeding along full throttle at high speeds. Her mind is remarkable in its proficiency and productivity; I am frequently amazed at the amount of work she can accomplish in a single day. But her racing thoughts, in all their usefulness, came at a cost. When it was time to unwind and slow down at the end of the day, her busy brain was no longer a blessing. Rather, it felt like a curse that robbed her of much-needed rest. This pattern led to exhaustion, depression, anxiety, and—for both of us—increasing levels of tension.

On an average night while Jen and I were trying to fall asleep, I could almost hear her busy mind buzzing

Little did I understand just how profoundly appreciation would increase our sleep and transform our interactions.

along. She would toss and turn, trying to quiet the noise. Jen's body was exhausted, but her mind was speeding along, reviewing the day and planning the next day's schedule.

Out of concern for my wife, and partly out of selfish desperation for my own rest since I am a light sleeper, I was highly motivated to help my wife enjoy some much-needed shut-eye. What happened next would revolutionize our marriage.

The skill of appreciation is one of the best brain habits we can use in our relationships. After studying the effects of appreciation and gratitude, I knew an increase in these things would help my wife's brain calm down. Little did I understand just how profoundly appreciation would increase our sleep and transform our interactions. My plan was to experiment with an exercise we would eventually call "3x3x3."

We will soon try this exercise, but here is what Jen and I practice. First, we take turns sharing three things from our day that we appreciate. Second, we express three qualities we appreciate about each other, including examples of these qualities "in action." Finally, we highlight three qualities we appreciate about God, again using examples. *(You could also insert another topic of your choosing here.)* Each step would look like this:

- Appreciation about my day: "I enjoyed my walk this afternoon. It felt so good to get outside and move around. The birds were singing, and the breeze was refreshing . . ."
- Appreciation about my spouse: "I really appreciate your heart for hospitality. When our friend Helen came over this evening, you worked hard to prepare a meal that she would enjoy. I like how you care about the people in our life!"
- Appreciation about God: "I am thankful for God's patience with me. I feel like God continues to give me opportunities to grow which makes me feel loved."

The first night we tried this exercise while snuggling in bed. The effects of the interaction were immediate and profound, which surprised both of us. During the exercise, I could feel Jen's body begin to relax and her breathing slow down. By the end, both of us were smiling and feeling peaceful. The exercise took about ten minutes to complete. Within another ten minutes, Jen was fast asleep for the night. This ended up being one of the best nights of sleep she had in a long time.

For years, we have used this exercise to close our day. Every time, Jen falls asleep within minutes instead of hours. Don't simply take my word for the value of this exercise; try it yourself, and watch what happens!

EXERCISES FOR HABIT #3:
APPRECIATE DAILY

Welcome to the third round of exercises. If your marriage was a cellphone, these exercises would be the booster that increases your joy signal.

Appreciation transforms your marriage by training your brain to focus on and amplify the good things in your environment, life, and relationships. The lack of appreciation leads to discontentment, criticism, and resentment. Appreciation activates the relational engine in your brain so that you can be your best relational self with your beloved.

Activating an "appreciation file" in the brain not only turns on our relational circuits, it allows our brain the opportunity to release "feel good" chemicals with the hormones dopamine, oxytocin, and serotonin—as well as endorphins, which make us feel alive. Our brain responds as though *we are living the moment all over again* when we "pull up," activate, and remember an appreciation memory. We amplify joy as we remember, feel, and share the special moment with our beloved. Also, we boost oxytocin levels when we *add touch into the equation*, so here is an opportunity to open a joy file and reap the reward.

Triple Your Joy ⏱ 15 MIN

> Here is your opportunity to practice the exercise that transformed my marriage and led to some really good sleep.

1. While holding hands or cuddling, take turns practicing the following steps. Be sure you both practice the first step before moving on. Include *daily examples* for each appreciation step if possible.
   Appreciation from my day: Share three highlights from your day.
   Appreciation for my beloved: Share three things you appreciate about your spouse.
   Appreciation for God (or your topic of choice): Share three things you appreciate about this topic. ⏱ 10 MIN
2. Discuss what you notice after practicing appreciation. ⏱ 3 MIN
3. Close with several minutes of quiet cuddling and resting together. ⏱ 2 MIN

Remember the Joy ⏱ 15 MIN

1. Take some time to cuddle or hold hands and reminisce about special trips and shared mo-

ments together over the course of your married life. Be sure to include:

Your thoughts and feelings at the time.

The factors that made these moments special for you. ⏱ **8 MIN**

2. Express some qualities you enjoy about your spouse so your spouse can hear. ⏱ **4 MIN**

3. Close with several minutes of quiet cuddling and resting together. ⏱ **3 MIN**

Go out for Joy ⏱ 15 MIN

Go out and do something fun that is relational and interactive. This needs to be an activity you both enjoy, and you need to be able to see and hear your spouse. You can go bowling, have a picnic, eat dinner at a new restaurant, go ice-skating, go bird watching, take an evening stroll through the park, go hiking, visit a flower nursery, sit at a coffee shop, etc.

During your outing, do all that you can to enjoy each other's presence, hold hands as much as possible, smile, laugh, and have fun.

1. Make it a point to review historic joy moments while planning future joy opportunities.

Historic joy is reviewing special moments where you felt loved and cared for by your spouse.

EXAMPLE: *When you brought me coffee this morning while I was running late, I felt loved and cared for.*

Future joy is thinking of and planning ways to continue increasing relational joy in your marriage.

EXAMPLE: *I would like us to end our days by sharing appreciation and to have a date night every other week.* ⏱ **8 MIN**

2. Discuss what was special about this exercise, then close your evening with quiet cuddling and resting. ⏱ **7 MIN**

CHAPTER 7

Habit #4: Nurture a Rhythm

THE FIRST AND SIMPLEST reason the joy gap starts to expand is tiredness. It is hard to build joy when you feel worn out and lack margin. For many couples, the idea of adding joy exercises for even fifteen minutes a day feels like more than they have the capacity to do.

Perhaps the core reason we lack margin in our lives is that we lack rhythm. Without a relational rhythm, our souls begin to wilt. When we can't find time for the kinds of activities that build joy and nurture the soul, life starts to feel overwhelming.

I have some good friends whose joy in marriage has seen them through a lot of hard times. They have developed several practices that have helped them establish a rhythm of relational connection. First, they eat breakfast together almost every morning. The husband is an early riser and loves to watch the sun light up the mountains near their home as they go from black to purple to pink. Once his wife is up, he sits at the table with her. They read the day's editorial from the newspaper and discuss it before getting on with the rest of their day. In the evenings, they sit in the living room together and enjoy a glass of wine. There is usually an animal on each of their laps. They take at least half an hour downloading their day and just enjoy being together.

My friend told me his philosophy. It is pretty simple. "You develop an affection for what you appreciate." Appreciation leads to affection, and affection leads to more appreciation. It becomes a cycle. It is this cycle of relational appreciation and affection that leads to a rhythm that creates margin in our lives, allowing us to be happy together in times of rest as well as times of activity.

JOY CAMP

Have you ever been camping? I am personally not much of a camper. I got tired of the mosquito bites and lack of sleep. But I have friends who are avid campers. One of them is Jim Wilder. He introduced me to a camping analogy for how to create rhythm in our marriages. He calls this analogy "joy camp."

Suppose a few families decide to spend a weekend in the mountains. The first thing they do is set up their campsite. They will likely set up a fire pit, pitch their tents, and hang their food up in the trees just outside the sleeping area to discourage unwanted visits from bears in the middle of the night.

Next, the adults will set up some ground rules. The youngest children have to stay with their parents near the campsite. The older kids can go down to the lake, but they need to wear life preservers to go out on the boat. Everyone else is free to explore the area and spend the day enjoying (and sometimes conquering) nature. One firm rule is also put in place. Everyone has to be back by 8 p.m. Camp won't be very joyful if 8:00 rolls around and people are missing. With those ground rules in place, people are free to start their adventure.

As the day winds down and people make their way back to camp, another kind of activity takes place. Meals are cooked. Drinks are served. A fire is built. People gather together to tell stories and share the adventures of the day. It doesn't matter whether you conquered nature or nature conquered you; at the end of the day, you get to be with your people, in joy camp, sharing the experience together.

This is the way life is supposed to work. We start our day in joy camp and end our day in joy camp. It doesn't matter whether your day is good or bad; you have the security of knowing you will be with people who are happy to see you at the end of the day. Families that successfully build this type of rhythm will find themselves living with the margin they need to handle the stresses of life and increase their joy.

To take this illustration a step further, imagine what happens if 8:00 p.m. arrives and two people are missing. What happens when 8:20 p.m. rolls around and they are still missing? There is not going to be nearly as much joy in the camp until everyone is accounted for. In the same way, when our family becomes a joy camp, no one is totally happy until everyone is back and connected and glad to be together. We want both husband and wife to be present and relationally engaged. We want the kids to be home and safe. We have that "no man left behind" mentality that isn't satisfied until everyone is in joy camp and relationally connected after a long day.

In today's world, families that function like joy camps are extremely rare. We have created a very isolated culture. Families no longer eat meals together. They don't tell each other stories of the day or take time to sit outside as the sun sets. Kids go to school, play sports, do homework, listen to their music, watch TV, and go to bed texting with friends. Even husbands and wives often don't connect until they are in bed, and even then, it happens as they are watching TV.

Building a habit of nurturing your soul through rhythm means turning your home into a joy camp where people know there will be a rhythm of relational time together. As you learn to start your day relationally, end your day relationally, and schedule regular times for relational connection, your capacity for joy will dramatically increase and your margin for rest will follow suit.

THE HAPPIEST PLACE ON EARTH

Rhythm is crucial to emotional capacity. If you don't get enough rest, everything about handling our emotions and relationships gets harder. In a recent poll, Denmark was voted the happiest place in the world to live.[1] In fact, it routinely ranks in the top five happiest countries in the world. One reason for this is its balance between work and relational connection.[2] The people of Denmark do a great job of nurturing a rhythm that creates the margin needed to enjoy life.

> *It is no accident that relational happiness and relational rhythm go hand in hand.*

Denmark's consistently high ranking has generally been attributed to a practice called *hygge* (pronounced hoo-guh). It can be defined as "intentional intimacy,"[3] and basically means doing things you like with people you like. One of the impacts of this lifestyle is lower stress because you rarely have to endure hardship alone. Knowing that you and "your people" are going to get together every week helps build relational and emotional capacity.

It is no accident that relational happiness and relational rhythm go hand in hand. Couples who succeed in creating a rhythm built around relationship and rest find the margin they need to live with less stress and more joy.

SHRINKING THE GAP

Having a routine to start and end your day nurtures a rhythm that naturally gives you margin. Learning to build routines that allow for rest as well as play creates a great environment for building joy. It is like working out at the gym. You don't actually grow muscles while you lift weights. Your muscles grow during the times of rest in between workouts. If you push yourself constantly without rest, you can actually diminish the results you get. In the same way, joy grows best when there is a rhythm of high activity (whether work or play) as well as low, restful activity.

EXERCISES FOR HABIT #4: NURTURE A RHYTHM

Welcome to the fourth and final round of exercises. Finding a good rhythm for our marriage comes down to two simple ingredients: *attention* and *timing*. Just like the eye smiles exercise teaches us, there is a time for connection and a time to rest. Knowing what time it is and paying attention to the fluctuating needs in your marriage will establish security and increase marriage joy.

Alternating joy and rest requires a rhythm where we stay attentive to ever-changing needs and respond at the right times. This is the rhythm we learn early on because, initially, caregivers and loved ones recognized when it was time for food, play, connection, or rest. In a healthy environment, the resources and the responses were there at just the right time in the right amount. This process established an unshakable security within us, a firm foundation we build on throughout our lifetime.

Unfortunately, the painful absence of timely attention and response to our needs during childhood instills fear and insecurity that leaves us feeling inadequate and uncertain. A disjointed rhythm develops, and our joy and rest sequence falls out of sync. As a result, we may avoid rest states later in life or develop dangerously low levels of joy. This deficiency makes us vulnerable to artificial, nonrelational means of compensating.

The following exercises focus on restoring an enjoyable rhythm that merges high-energy joy with low-energy rest.

Rest and Joy ⏱ 15 MIN

> Joy grows better after rest. The inability to quiet is one of the greatest threats to your emotional and mental health. The lack of rest pokes a hole in the "joy balloon" of marriage. For this exercise, you and your partner will first calm your bodies and minds, then shift to joy. You can play calming music in the background if you prefer.

1. Get comfortable so you do not need to support any part of your body. You can lie down on the floor or a couch. ⏱ 1 MIN

2. Scan your body and see where you feel tense or stiff. ⏱ 1 MIN

3. Take some deep breaths from your belly, then tighten your whole body. Begin to relax, starting with your face, then neck, shoulders, back, hands, arms, stomach, buttocks, legs, feet, and finally, toes. Try several rounds of this body quieting sequence. ⏱ 2 MIN

4. After some time spent tightening and releasing your muscles, scan your body again to see what you notice. ⏱ 1 MIN

5. Share with your partner what you are feeling. ⏱ 1 MIN

6. Position yourselves so your knees are touching, and hold hands. Briefly share three things you feel thankful for today. ⏱ 4 MIN

7. Next, while still holding hands, practice the eye smiles exercise from chapter 4. ⏱ 2 MIN

8. Discuss what you notice after trying these steps, and close with quiet cuddling and resting. ⏱ 3 MIN

Finding Your Marriage Flavor ⏱ 15 MIN

1. Start by sharing highlights from your day. Once
    you feel relational, discuss the following topics.
    What we like: What do you like about your
    marriage? How does this make you feel? (*This is
    not a time to use the word "but" or stir up what
    annoys you about your marriage.*)
    EXAMPLE: *I like that we value quality time. It
    makes me feel encouraged thinking about how
    we protect opportunities to connect with each
    other and the people we love.*
    Who we are: Talk about the unique flavor in
    your marriage. What important qualities are
    present in your marriage? What specific quali-
    ties are meaningful for you?
    EXAMPLE: *I like that we are people who value rela-
    tionships, and we prioritize time with each other
    and with friends.*
    Looking back: When the day comes and you
    are at the end of your life, what things would
    you like said about how you valued your mar-
    riage? What would you like to be able to say
    about how you cultivated and tended your mar-
    riage? In other words, what kind of marriage
    legacy do you want to have?
    EXAMPLE: *I want to say that I finished well and I
    loved my spouse with all my heart. I want my*

loved ones to recognize that I deeply valued my marriage. ⏱ **9 MIN**

2. Practice the eye smiles exercise for a joy and rest sequence. Remember to look away when you feel the joy is no longer growing. ⏱ **3 MIN** Note: *You can play music if you like.*

3. Discuss what you noticed about this exercise, then close with quiet cuddling and resting. ⏱ **3 MIN**

Wrap Up:
Making a PLAN

WE STARTED THIS BOOK with the promise that investing fifteen minutes a day to do the exercises in our joy workout program and doing them for at least thirty days would lead to a noticeable growth in the joy in your marriage. The more consistent you are, the more quickly these exercises will lead to new habits. We hope you have been doing the exercises, but perhaps you just read the book and skipped the exercises. That sounds like something we would have done. We encourage you to go back through the book with your husband or your wife and do the exercises. Remember, your relational brain benefits from practice and interaction, not information. If you are intentional about following the PLAN, you will start building new habits that will help you find the joy you need to deal with all the hard stuff life throws at you.

Take some time to review with your spouse how you felt when you first started this book and where you are today. What changes have you noticed?

As you prepare your own plan for moving forward, let's review the four habits taught in this book.

P: Play together. Don't let your marriage become all business and avoidance. Use the exercises provided to plan out some fun activities to do together.

L: Listen for emotion. Training yourself to listen with your right brain first instead of your left brain takes practice for most of us. Take advantage of the exercises in the book to practice identifying and validating the SAD-SAD emotions your partner feels.

A: Appreciate daily. Left-brain dominant people are often good at gratitude but not so good at appreciation. Begin building an arsenal of appreciation strategies that focus on your partner. Collect lists. Write stories. Build libraries of music, movies, or books you both enjoy. Be creative as you grow the practice of sharing appreciation with each other, and remember—appreciation attracts; resentment repels.

N: Nurture rhythm. Turn your home into a joy camp. This won't happen overnight, but follow some of the suggested guidelines and start creating a rhythm that keeps the marriage connected, especially in the evening hours. The stronger the relational routine you are able to build, the more emotionally stable your home will be and the more opportunities for joy you will have.

MAKING YOUR OWN PLAN

Now that you have been through the material, take some time as a couple to write out your plan for moving forward. Here are some steps to consider:

- Decide the best time of day for doing exercises together.
- Select some of your favorite exercises from this book, and make up some of your own.
- Get out your calendar and decide how often you can have date nights, go to special events, and schedule getaways together.
- Write a letter every New Year's Eve to document how your partner has brought joy to your life that year and what your hopes and dreams are for your future together. (You can also do this every quarter.)

We encourage you to get out your calendar and put your plan in writing. You can think of these exercises as a diet plan for your marriage. Only, instead of shrinking your waistline, you are shrinking your joy gap. Whenever you feel like you need a refresher, you can get out the book and go through the plan again.

FINAL THOUGHTS

No marriage is perfect, but if you build enough joy in your relationship, you will recover from conflict more quickly, feel greater security in your relationship, and find yourself looking forward to time together more often.

One of the most powerful things you can do in this life is have a great marriage. Think about it. Marriage is a punchline for comedians. People have learned to expect that marriage is a trial to endure. But imagine the impact on our society if joy became the common experience of married couples everywhere! We would see less anger, less anxiety, and better relationships. Our world could use a joy revolution, don't you think? It starts one marriage at a time.

We hope this book has helped you shrink the joy gap in your marriage and helped you set sail on a new adventure of building a joy-filled marriage. Just a reminder: There is more fun to be had! The appendices contain more exercises that you can use to continue building joy in your marriage.

More "Play Together" Exercises

Expressing Your Joy ⏱ 15 MIN

The brain processes nonverbal cues faster than words. This is why, "It's not *what* you said, it's *how* you said it!" carries so much weight in conversation. As I say in my book *Transforming Fellowship*,

> Eye contact, facial expressions, voice tone (prosody), posture, gestures, timing and intensity all contribute to the interactive dance we know as communication. . . . Our body is the canvas to express our thoughts, feelings, desires, fears and our most prized memories. . . . When working together, our brain and body tell a story that shows up on our face and in our voice.[1]

For this exercise, you first engage the nonverbal brain in order to activate joy in your relationship.

1. While cuddling or holding hands, individually think about the first time you met your spouse. What was happening? What were you thinking and feeling? ⏱ **2 MIN**

2. Now, take turns nonverbally "telling" the story about the time you first met your spouse. Using your face, body, motions, and gestures, convey what was happening in the story including what you were thinking and feeling. Be creative and have fun. ⏱ **4 MIN**

3. When you finish your nonverbal story, tell the story again using words while you demonstrate it. ⏱ **6 MIN**

4. Once you both finish telling your stories, spend some time cuddling or holding hands, then discuss what you enjoyed about this exercise. Close with quiet cuddling and resting together. ⏱ **3 MIN**

Get More Relational ⏱ **15 MIN**

1. Take turns massaging each other. You can start with your partner's neck, shoulders, arms, hands, back, etc. While you massage your partner, emphasize the qualities you enjoy about your partner so he or she can hear. ⏱ **10 MIN**

HINT: *You may want to set a timer so each person receives the same amount of time.*

2. Share how this exercise felt for you. ⏱ **2 MIN**

3. Practice several minutes of quiet cuddling and resting together. ⏱ **3 MIN**

Interactive Adventure ⏱ 15 MIN

For this exercise, you and your spouse need to do something fun that engages your body and your relational brain.

1. Try an activity that is both fun and interactive, such as flying a kite, throwing a Frisbee, playing ping-pong or hacky-sack, painting or drawing, giving piggyback rides, riding bicycles, walking a trail, or playing miniature golf or charades. ⏱ **12 MIN**

   NOTE: *The goal here is to have fun and smile, not win.*

2. At the end of the activity, spend some time cuddling or holding hands and discuss what you enjoyed about this interaction. ⏱ **3 MIN**

More "Listen for Emotion" Exercises

Satisfaction from My Week ⏱ 15 MIN

Learning satisfaction is an important childhood maturity skill that, when present, anchors our marriages and when absent, adds unnecessary friction and tension. When couples know what satisfies, they keep joy levels high and minimize marriage discontentment. When our brain notices what is satisfying from our interactions, we are more likely to notice emotions that are present in each other and ourselves.

1. Take turns remembering three to five things that were satisfying and fulfilling as well as three to five things that were not very satisfying

from your week. You can write your lists down or type them on your phone. ⏱ **3 MIN**

SATISFYING EXAMPLES:

It was satisfying to enjoy such beautiful weather this week.

It was satisfying to watch a movie last night with my entire family.

Going out to lunch with my coworkers for a birthday celebration was enjoyable. The interactions were deeply satisfying.

NOT-SO-SATISFYING EXAMPLES:

It was not satisfying when my dog chewed my shoe on Monday.

I did not enjoy running out of milk this morning for my cereal.

It was not satisfying when my teenage son left the house without saying goodbye last night.

2. When your lists are complete, one of you read your satisfying list. ⏱ **1 MIN**

3. After reading the satisfying list, the listener validates the emotions that were present. ⏱ **1 MIN**

4. Next, the reader shares the not-so-satisfying list, and the listener validates emotions that were expressed. ⏱ **2 MIN**

5. Before moving on, take a moment of rest while you cuddle. ⏱ **2 MIN**

6. Switch roles, and follow the same sequence. ⏱ **4 MIN**

7. Briefly discuss what you noticed from this exercise, then close with quiet cuddling and resting together. ⏱ **2 MIN**

Validation and Comfort ⏱ 15 MIN

Validation looks at how big the negative emotion is in your partner, and you say what you see and hear. We stay tender toward each other's weaknesses. As Marcus said earlier, the caution here is not to try and fix our spouse; rather, join him or her in the feelings.

Validation = *I see you are bothered about this problem. This is very upsetting for you!*

Comfort = *I am glad I can be here with you. What can you find in this situation to feel thankful for?*

1. Start by sharing a few highlights from your day. This step warms up your brain's relational circuits. ⏱ **2 MIN**

2. Next, pick a recent situation that was difficult or intimidating for you, but keep it at a moderate level of emotion so it's not too intense. Take turns sharing your story with your spouse. ⏱ **2 MIN**

    EXAMPLE: *My boss at work ignored me today when I tried to talk with her about my concern. I felt hurt and minimized.*

3. When you hear your spouse share the situation, respond by validating the emotion (say what you see and hear), then offer comfort, highlighting something to appreciate in the midst of the emotions. ⏱ 1 MIN

   EXAMPLE: *I can see this really bothered you. I would be hurt by this as well!* (Validation) *I am glad you shared this with me. Thankfully, Mike was there to encourage you afterwards. What else can you think of to appreciate?* (Comfort)

4. When you both finish, talk about how this exercise felt for you. ⏱ 2 MIN

5. Now it is time to shift gears with a bit of joy. Take 30 seconds to remember the highlights from your day, then sit across from each other knee to knee while you hold hands. Without using words, practice eye smiles. Look at each other with warm smiles, joy, and love, then look away to rest. (You can play music if you like.) ⏱ 3 MIN

6. Next, take turns sharing three qualities you admire in your spouse. ⏱ 3 MIN

7. Close with quiet cuddling and resting together. ⏱ 2 MIN

Increasing My Marriage Intelligence ⏱ 15 MIN

Validation and comfort help us feel seen, understood, and connected. One of the common reasons VCR fails is because we do not recognize a specific emotion in our spouse. We then do not first validate his or her feelings. Continue to bolster your brain's ability to recognize emotions in your spouse.

1. Briefly share what you are thankful for today. ⏱ 2 MIN

2. Next, take turns nonverbally conveying what you feel when you encounter each of the following emotions (see list below). Think about what is happening in your body when you feel each emotion. Use eye contact, facial expressions, vocal expressions, posture, gestures, timing, and intensity to fully convey your emotion and, as always, have some fun! NOTE: *You may want to stand in order to get your body involved in this exercise.* ⏱ 7 MIN

   Joy: *I am glad to be with you!*

   Sadness: *I lost something that brings me joy.*

   Anxiety: *I fear I may not find joy as I look into the future.*

   Despair: *I feel like joy is impossible for me. I lack the time and resources to fix a problem that keeps robbing my joy.*

Shame: *I feel like hiding because I am not bringing you joy.*

Anger: *I want something to stop because it is robbing my joy.*

Disgust: *I want to get away from that which is not life-giving and threatening my joy.*

3. After you both finish your examples, discuss what you noticed from this exercise. Include the following topics:

   What emotions tend to be hardest for you to personally navigate?

   What emotions are harder for you to recognize and stay connected with in your spouse?

   ⏱ 2 MIN

4. Share with your spouse what you enjoy about his/her face while you hold hands. When you finish, practice the eye smiles exercise. ⏱ 3 MIN

5. Close with quiet cuddling and resting together. ⏱ 1 MIN

More "Appreciate Daily" Exercises

Food and Joy ⏱ 15 MIN

During your wedding reception, you probably fed your new spouse a piece of cake. Some of you were feisty and smeared it on your beloved's face. Either way, wide smiles surely donned your faces. This exercise focuses on the feeding part of the fun—not so much the smearing! Meals are one of the best times to build joy. Eating together provides a golden opportunity to share the gift of your attention and connect with your mate. We now turn our sights to using this wonderful food and joy combination to spark smiles.

1. Start by sharing a few highlights from your day. This warms up your brain's relational circuits. ⏱ 3 MIN

2. Take turns feeding each other a meal, snack, or dessert. Yes, this may feel awkward, but have fun and laugh. While you feed each other, express what you enjoy about each other, including how you feel your spouse "feeds you" spiritually, emotionally, mentally, physically, and relationally. ⏱ 8 MIN

3. Once you finish this interaction, talk about what you noticed from the experience. ⏱ 2 MIN

4. Close with quiet cuddling and resting together. ⏱ 2 MIN

Write Your Joy ⏱ 15 MIN

As Marcus said earlier, composing a love letter can be a meaningful activity that you will cherish for years to come. This heartfelt exchange provides an opportunity to express your heart and share your love the old-fashioned way. You will need paper and pen for this exercise.

1. Take a moment to think about what you love about your spouse, then write your spouse a love letter. While this doesn't have to be volumes of books, it does need to be longer than three sentences. Take the necessary time to complete this task. ⏱ 6 MIN

2. When finished, take turns reading your love letter to your spouse. ⏱ **6 MIN**

3. Discuss what you enjoyed about this exercise, then close with quiet cuddling and resting. ⏱ **3 MIN**

Run for Joy ⏱ **15 MIN**

Our nervous system cycles between high energy and low energy states. Some of us tend to be high-energy responders who prefer activity, motion, and movement. We pursue activities that get our adrenaline pumping. Some of us are low-energy responders who prefer restful and soothing activities. We like our quiet time with a cup of tea and soft music. It helps to identify the preferences of our nervous system so we can plan activities that best match the needs and styles in our marriage.

One way to better gauge and identify our preferences is by looking at our response to feeling shame. Low-energy responders tend to *beat themselves up* when they feel ashamed: "I can't do anything right! I am such a fool!" High-energy responders, however, tend to *beat other people up* when they feel shame: "You can't do anything right! You are such a fool!" While we may relate to both reactions, we all tend to lean toward one style. Low-energy responders can be quick to blame themselves while high-energy responders can be quick to blame other people. Now let's practice the exercise to see what best fits you and your spouse.

1. Discuss your preferences to see if you lean more toward high-energy activities such as walks, runs, bike rides, hiking, and fast-paced exercise, or low-energy activities such as sitting in a quiet place with soft music, playing chess, or reading a book. For example, if you had the option of choosing an early morning walk or sitting in a chair watching the sunset, which would you prefer? ⏱ 3 MIN

2. Put your thoughts to the test with the following experiment. Take a few minutes to try a high-energy activity such as doing jumping jacks, stretching exercises, sit-ups, walking, or riding bikes around your neighborhood. While you move, discuss some of your favorite shared memories such as vacations, trips, birthdays, holidays, etc. ⏱ 4 MIN

3. Next, make yourselves comfortable on a couch or a recliner while you play soft music in the background. Continue to reminisce more of your favorite shared memories. These interactions do not need to be long. ⏱ 4 MIN

4. Discuss this exercise and share what you notice. How can you use this information in your marriage? ⏱ **2 MIN**

5. Close with quiet cuddling and resting together. ⏱ **2 MIN**

More "Nurture a Rhythm" Exercises

Resting and Kissing ⏱ 15 MIN

Shortening the window of time between moments of shared joy requires us to notice that joy and rest are needed, and then practice strategic rhythms to increase the joy.

1. Make yourselves comfortable and spend some time resting as you cuddle.

   NOTE: *Keep this nonverbal to enhance the bonding experience. You can set a timer if you like.*
   ⏱ 3 MIN

2. Holding hands and looking at each other, take turns telling your spouse the qualities you first observed in him or her that made you fall in

love. Include examples where you saw these qualities in action. ⏱ **5 MIN**

3. Next, position yourselves knee to knee and hold hands. Practice eye smiles for a joy and rest sequence. Remember to look away at the right times when you feel the joy is no longer growing.

   NOTE: *You can play music if you like.* ⏱ **3 MIN**

4. Kiss each other like you mean it, then discuss what you notice from this joy and rest sequence. ⏱ **2 MIN**

5. Close with quiet cuddling and resting together. ⏱ **2 MIN**

More Bedroom Joy ⏱ 15 MIN

You will want some privacy for this exercise.

1. While lying in bed holding each other, practice the following sequence.

   First, use quiet, soothing touch to comfort and relax your spouse while you tell your spouse what you enjoy about his or her character and personality.

   Next, use high-energy stimulating touch to arouse your spouse while you share what you like about his or her body.

   Now return to rest using soothing touch while you share the ways your spouse makes you feel loved and valued.

Use high-energy, stimulating touch to arouse your spouse while you affirm your love and desire for your beloved. ⏱ **9 MIN**
(As much time as you need!) Enjoy relational intimacy that makes you both smile.

2. Share appreciation or pray, thanking God for your partner, so your partner can hear. ⏱ **3 MIN**

3. Spend some time resting together with quiet cuddling. ⏱ **3 MIN**

Using Your Joy Senses ⏱ 15 MIN

We now practice an exercise designed to maximize marriage joy using your five senses.

1. **Sight**: You see because your eyes translate light into images the brain can process via the optic nerve. Sit across from each other while you hold hands. Tell your beloved what you like about him or her as you peer into your beloved's eyes. Include qualities you can see as you look at your spouse. ⏱ **2 MIN**

2. **Sound**: Through a complex series of steps, your outer and inner ear work together to funnel sound waves that turn into vibrations that your cochlear nerve receives and then sends to the brain for processing. Hold each other and take turns placing your head on your spouse's chest. With your eyes closed, listen to your spouse as

he or she tells you the things you do that make him or her feel loved, special, and appreciated. ⏱ **3 MIN**

3. **Smell**: Nerve receptors located in your nasal cavity pick up chemicals in the air which trigger a response that sends information to the brain for processing via the olfactory nerve. Smell is one of the fastest ways to trigger an old memory. While cuddling and holding each other, lean into each other's necks and take several moments to quietly rest as you breathe in the scent of your spouse. When finished, share how his or her familiar smell brings you comfort.
   NOTE: *You may want to be sure this step doesn't happen after a sweaty workout, so take the appropriate steps to keep joy levels high.* ⏱ **3 MIN**

4. **Taste**: Thanks to small bumps on your tongue called papillae, chemicals from the food you eat go to your taste buds, which stimulate special cells that activate receptors and signals. These signals are then sent for processing. Close your eyes and tenderly kiss your spouse, then share what you enjoy about kissing your beloved.
   NOTE: *As a friendly reminder, Marcus and I suggest you avoid a meal containing onions and garlic before you practice this step.* ⏱ **3 MIN**

5. **Touch**: Your skin has three layers, and receptor

cells embedded in these layers send signals to the brain for evaluation. Some areas of the body have more and different kinds of receptors, so certain areas of your beloved's body are more sensitive than other areas. Touch your beloved's face and body and describe what you feel. Enhance this step by closing your eyes. NOTE: *If you feel adventurous, alternate touch that calms your spouse with touch that excites your spouse.* ⏱ 3 MIN

6. Discuss whether you prefer one sense over another as you cuddle together. ⏱ 1 MIN

Fun with Friends ⏱ 15 MIN

Here is a chance to have fun while you share some joy with your friends. Creating a narrative (telling a story) helps your brain add more value to something important to you and it gives your brain the opportunity to spread joy.

Go on a date with another couple. Tell some stories, share what you learned from this book, and invite them to try one of the four habits: Appreciate Daily.

1. Before practicing, highlight the effect on your marriage from learning the material and trying the four habits. As an example, you may want

to share your favorite exercises from the book and explain why these were helpful for you. ○ **5 MIN**

2. Give your friends the opportunity to enjoy the power of appreciation by doing the following exercise during your time together. Follow the steps below, and be sure each person has the chance to contribute.

Share three highlights from your week.

Share three qualities you enjoy about your spouse.

Share three characteristics you appreciate in the other couple.

Share what you notice after you practice this appreciation exercise.

For homework in the comfort of your own home, talk with your spouse about what you enjoyed from your date night, then close with quiet cuddling and resting together. ○ **10 MIN**

Congratulations on the completion of your exercises! You have worked hard to get here. Marcus and I encourage you to continue practicing the exercises and insert the habits into your daily life and routine. Discuss pitfalls you predict that lie ahead as you begin to walk this out. Schedule time in your day and week for joyful connection. Protect your time before bed to discuss the day and address any problems *before* you climb into bed so your bedroom remains a haven for joy and rest. Marcus and I celebrate your success and pray that joy will blossom in your marriage.

Additional Resources

Chris Coursey, *Transforming Fellowship: 19 Brain Skills That Build Joyful Community* (Holland, MI: Coursey Creations, LLC, 2016).

Chris and Jen Coursey, *30 Days of Joy for Busy Married Couples* (Holland, MI: Coursey Creations, LLC, 2013).

C. Coursey, E. Khouri, S. Sutton & E. J. Wilder, *Joy Starts Here: The Transformation Zone* (East Peoria, IL: Shepherd's House, 2013).

Marcus Warner and Jim Wilder, *Rare Leadership: Four Uncommon Habits for Increasing Trust, Joy, and Engagement in the People You Lead* (Chicago: Moody Publishers, 2015).

Marcus Warner, *Slaying the Monster: Six Battle Strategies for Overcoming Pornography* (Carmel, IN: Deeper Walk International, 2016).

Marcus Warner, *Understanding the Wounded Heart* (Carmel, IN: Deeper Walk International, 2013).

The 4 Habits of Joy-Filled Marriages: A Small Group Curriculum from Thrive Today and Deeper Walk International, featuring the authors and their wives. Coming Fall of 2019.

Gary Chapman, *The 5 Love Languages: The Secret to Love That Lasts* (Chicago: Northfield, 2015).

Find useful resources to build the joy that fuels a happy marriage at **HappyHappyMarriage.org**

Acknowledgments

CHRIS AND MARCUS would like to say a special word of thanks to Duane Sherman for reaching out to us with the concept for this book. We also want to acknowledge the influence and inspiration of our friend and colleague, Dr. Jim Wilder. This book started by interacting with Jim about brain science, joy, and its application to marriage. We both owe Jim a great debt for his guidance through the years.

Of course, we also want to thank our wives for putting up with being illustrations in a book on marriage and supporting us throughout this process.

Notes

INTRODUCTION

1. For more information on how joy functions as the brain's ideal fuel, see Marcus Warner and Jim Wilder, *Rare Leadership: 4 Uncommon Habits for Increasing Trust, Joy, and Engagement in the People You Lead* (Chicago: Moody Publishers, 2016).

2. This story has been adapted from one in E. James Wilder et al., *Joy Starts Here: The Transformation Zone* (East Peoria, IL: Shepherd's House, 2013), 24–25.

3. This quote came from a personal email to the author.

CHAPTER 1–SHRINK YOUR JOY GAP

1. Dopamine is the hormone that makes you feel happy. However, the rush only lasts as long as the hormone is active, and it doesn't do much to help you form attachments because it can be produced by all sorts of experiences. Oxytocin is sometimes called "the love hormone" because it makes you feel connected and glad to be together. It is primarily activated by contact with one particular person, thus helping us bond to that person.

CHAPTER 2–THE BRAIN SCIENCE BEHIND JOY

1. Attachment theory has essentially become the cornerstone of child-hood development theory. For an excellent overview of the role of attachment, trauma, and maturity development, we recommend *The Life Model* which was developed at Shepherd's House Counseling Center in Van Nuys, California, under the guidance of Dr. Jim Wilder.

2. Yale Divinity School has started an annual conference on the theology of joy. *Psychology Today* magazine is filled with articles on the subject, e.g., Emma M. Seppälä, "The Science behind the Joy of Sharing Joy," *Psychology Today*, July 15, 2013, https://www.psychologytoday.com/us/blog/feeling-it/201307/the-science-behind-the-joy-sharing-joy.

3. The brain magnet refers to the nucleus acumbens, the thalamus, and the neurocircuitry that connects your limbic system to the brain. The nucleus acumbens is the pain and pleasure center of the brain. It feels a rush with connection to someone we love. However, it can also feel like you are going to die when it doesn't get what it wants.

4. This part of your brain is called the right orbital prefrontal cortex and is located just behind your right eye.

5. See Marcus Warner and Jim Wilder, *Rare Leadership: 4 Uncommon Habits for Increasing Trust, Joy, and Engagement in the People You Lead* (Chicago: Moody Publishers, 2016) for a complete explanation of these four uncommon habits.

6. Karl Lehman, *Outsmarting Yourself: Catching Your Past Invading the Present and What to Do about It* (Libertyville, IL: This Joy! Books, 2011).

7. For a more complete overview, see Warner and Wilder, *Rare Leadership* or Chris Coursey, *Transforming Fellowship* (Scotts Valley, CA: CreateSpace Independent Publishing Platform, 2018) on nineteen relational skills that are anchored in brain science.

CHAPTER 3–WHY JOY CAN BE SO HARD TO FIND

1. For more information on master marriages and disaster marriages, visit http://gottman.com.

CHAPTER 4–HABIT #1: PLAY TOGETHER

1. This couple has written a book on marriage and ministry. See Tom and Sandi Blaylock, *Marriage on Mission: How Strengthening Your Marriage Multiplies Your Missional Impact* (n.p.: Missional Challenge, 2016).
2. We explained relational circuits in chapter 2.

CHAPTER 5–HABIT #2: LISTEN FOR EMOTION

1. The Smalley Institute website advertises this DVD set as "the bestselling relationship video series of all time!" It was originally released as a VHS series called "Hidden Keys to Loving Relationships" in 1993 by Gary Smalley Seminars, Inc.
2. Unprocessed pain often comes from implicit memories. For more about this process, see Lehman, *Outsmarting Yourself*. You can learn more about mindsight with the work of Dr. Daniel Siegel who first came up with the term "mindsight" to describe our ability to perceive another person's mind. http://drdansiegel.com.

CHAPTER 6–HABIT #3: APPRECIATE DAILY

1. Prathik Kini, Joel Wong, Sydney McInnis, Nicole Gabana, Joshua W. Brown, "In the News: Gratitude," https://www.indiana.edu/~irf/home/in-the-news/.
2. Dr. Christian Jarrett, "How Expressing Gratitude Might Change Your Brain," January 12, 2016, https://www.aol.com/article/2016/01/12/how-expressing-gratitude-might-change-your-brain/21295708/.

CHAPTER 7–HABIT #4: NURTURE A RHYTHM

1. According to both the 2013 and 2016 World Happiness Report, Denmark was the world's happiest country. Oliver Smith, "Denmark Regains Title of 'World's Happiest Country,'" March 16, 2016, https://www.telegraph.co.uk/travel/news/denmark-regains-title-of-happiest-country/.
2. "Denmark has the best work-life balance in Europe," http://studyindenmark.dk/news/denmark-has-the-best-work-life-balance-in-europe.

3. Marie Helweg-Larsen, "Why Denmark Dominates the World Happiness Report Rankings Year after Year," March 20, 2018, https://theconversation.com/why-denmark-dominates-the-world-happiness-report-rankings-year-after-year-93542.

APPENDIX 1

1. Chris Coursey, *Transforming Fellowship* (Scotts Valley, CA: CreateSpace Independent Publishing Platform, 2018), 140–41.

Habits are formed in *community*.

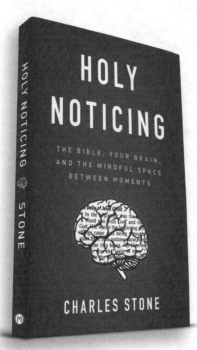

SIMPLE IDEAS, LASTING LOVE.

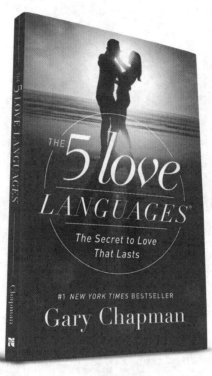